WHAT ARE YOU DOING, GOD?

A BOOK FOR ANYONE WHO HAS EVER QUESTIONED GOD

BO ORTEGO

BO ORTEGO

Copyright © 2021 Bo Ortego

The author has made every effort possible to check and ensure the accuracy of the information presented in this book. However, the information herein is sold without warranty, either expressed or implied. The author, publisher, nor any dealer or distributor of this book will be held liable for any damages caused either directly or indirectly by the instructions or information contained in this book.

In accordance with the U.S. Copyright Act of 1976, the scanning, uploading, and electronic sharing of any part of this book without the permission of the publisher is unlawful piracy and theft of the author's intellectual property. If you would like to use material from this book (other than for review purposes), prior written permission must be obtained by contacting the publisher. Thank you for your support of the author's rights.

Notice of Rights: All rights reserved. No part of this book may be reproduced or transmitted in any form by any means, electronic, mechanical, photocopy, recording, or other without the prior written permission of the publisher.

Permission: For information on getting permission for reprints and excerpts, contact: Bo Ortego at boortego.com or boortego@gmail.com

Unless otherwise noted, Scripture quotations are taken from The Holy Bible: English Standard Version. Copyright © 2001, 2016 by Crossway Bibles, a publishing ministry of Good News Publishers. All rights reserved.

Scripture quotations marked NIV are from The Holy Bible, New International Version. Copyright © 1973, 1978, 1984, 2011 by Zondervan, Biblica, Inc.™ All rights reserved worldwide.

ISBN 978-1-7365242-0-6 (eBook)

ISBN 978-1-7365242-1-3

CONTENTS

Introduction   v

1. Question   1
2. Directive   18
3. Promise   31
4. Plan   43
5. Patience   60
6. Pride   71
7. Faith   95
8. Prayer   112
9. Worship   128

Discussion Questions   145

INTRODUCTION

Have you ever questioned God or wanted to? If so, this book is for you. It is a book that explores what happened when a biblical prophet named Habakkuk did just that.

As I say this, you may think that is a strange topic to write a book on. Really, there is a part of me that actually agrees with you. When I decided to write a book, this topic wasn't the initial one. However, something changed along the way. While I believe there are many reasons this topic came to the forefront, maybe one of the biggest reasons was the global pandemic of 2020.

At the beginning of 2020, I was kicking around various ideas I wanted to turn into a book. As I was settling in on one, the pandemic hit. Life changed overnight for so many people. As I finish this book, it is the end of 2020, and there is still so much that isn't back to normal. Life has been dramatically altered, and there is no telling if things will ever go back to the way they were before.

As the weeks and months began to pass, I started to notice something. While many were trying so hard to get things under control and end this terrible pandemic, it seemed like there were always more questions than answers. Honestly, not only were the answers scarce, but the answers we had didn't seem to be all that great.

Now, that isn't meant to be a knock on the experts and those leading us through this unprecedented time. I can't imagine how difficult it was trying to lead the various efforts that were taking place, all intending to discover solutions to the rather unprecedented situation we all found ourselves in. Any critique of those efforts will be left to someone else.

Instead, I'm simply highlighting what happens all too often when things take an unexpected turn in our lives or society as a whole. We are left with questions, and we seek answers. This isn't rocket science; it is pretty basic stuff that I'll get into in the coming chapters.

The act of questioning our circumstances and what happens to us has always fascinated me, though. I'm not completely sure why, but I think it has something to do with the path my life took.

I've worked a lot of very interesting jobs over the years. I've spent my time in sales, retail, and other similar jobs like most people, but I've also worked at places that were a little more unique. For instance, I worked in the governor's office of a state I lived in previously and a juvenile detention facility. While there were other positions that could fall into this category, these two particularly stand out in my memory, especially as I talk about the act of questioning.

My job in the governor's office was to deal with people for the governor. It should come as no surprise that an elected official holding this level of office was not sitting around all day ready to handle calls and visits from the citizens. Still, you'd surprised how many times people asked me to let them speak to the governor.

As I started my time in that role, one thing became apparent very quickly—people rarely contact an elected official like their governor unless there is something wrong or they have a complaint. In no small part, my job in the office was to handle communication between the governor's office and the citizens, and most of my time was centered around listening to issues and giving an ear to the people to voice their complaints.

These complaints most often took the form of questioning me regarding a policy or why things were the way they were with respect to that person's situation. Unfortunately, I never had many answers, but it really began to open my eyes to how common it is for people to question things when faced with undesirable outcomes or situations.

Years later, I was a supervisor at a juvenile detention facility. It was quite a different context than the governor's office to be sure, but I was once again faced with constant questions. As the one calling the shots for the entire facility, there wasn't a day that would go by where a resident did not have a question for me regarding why he or she had to do something or couldn't do what they wanted. Again, things weren't what they wanted, so they questioned me. Unfortunately, just like when I worked in the governor's office, I often did not have answers that would satisfy them or alleviate their concerns.

I don't enjoy talking about the above examples from my work history in this context because I actually enjoy having answers to questions and tough topics. Really, it is something I am rather passionate about. I don't like having to tell people, "I don't know." I don't enjoy lacking an answer that would alleviate concerns or help a person through something difficult.

I'm a pastor now, and the job is something I love in large part because I get to help people. Specifically, the aspect of my job I enjoy the most is getting to help people grow in understanding more about God and His Word.

This playing itself out in different discipleship endeavors

has always been what gets me excited. When I first jumped into ministry many years ago, I found out very quickly this was my passion. I eventually went on to get two master's degrees and spent countless hours learning and working in other ways to better equip myself in order to help people grow in their faith and understanding of God.

Along the way, though, I realized something. There were endless instances when a good answer or solution to a person's problem was lacking. While I knew there wouldn't be some silver bullet that solved everything, I was rather surprised by how often the questions people had were left without adequate answers. Maybe I was just naive (and I certainly was for many years), but as I started down my ministry journey, I was sure there would be answers that could help most people in almost everything they faced. It was just my job to find them!

Boy, was I wrong! Maybe the most humbling thing for me as I matured in ministry is realizing there isn't a great answer for so much of what people face. While I am absolutely convinced so many of our day-to-day issues would either be alleviated or greatly diminished if we all simply remembered who our God was, what He has done for us, and what He has said in His Word, there are bigger issues and more difficult situations where answers seem sparse.

What do we do in those situations? How was I supposed to help people with questions stemming from those types of circumstances? While the Bible does not give detailed answers to all our questions, God did leave us something rather incredible—the book of Habakkuk. This book of the Bible is all about questioning God. It focuses on a prophet who is questioning the one he serves.

So while we may not always find the answers to our questions, through this Old Testament book, God has given us a blueprint to help us navigate through those times. I was blown away by this book when I studied it. I never knew God left this wonderful tool for His followers in order to help us navigate through those difficult times and seasons.

Unfortunately, I am not the only one who did not know this tool was available. I've talked to many Christians who either haven't thought much about this book of the Bible or even read it. What a shame! I am convinced of the truth regarding the sufficiency of Scripture (2 Tim. 3:16–17), and I believe the book of Habakkuk is something that, when understood, equips us to face those tough questions.

That is the purpose of this book—to help followers of God understand what He left for us through the book of Habakkuk. And as a result of the various lessons found within its chapters, we can all be better equipped to navigate through those times when we are facing situations and circumstances that cause us to question God.

This is my prayer for everyone who reads this work. I pray that you leave understanding more about our God, how great He truly is, and that He loved us enough to give us this book of the Bible in order to help during the hardest and darkest moments of our lives.

1

QUESTION

"What are you doing?" I think this is the question I have asked the most in my life. One of the reasons I keep asking this question is because I have worked with many kids over the years. Whether it was during my time in ministry or in other contexts, this question seemed to always fly out of my mouth when the actions of the kids were confusing, dangerous, or downright troubling.

If you have kids or worked with the age group I am describing, I'm sure you can relate. There were plenty of fun and memorable times, but there were also times where I was shocked by what was happening. Whether at church or in detention, they were always doing things that left me scratching my head. Their propensity to push the envelope on rules or creatively find a way around them has always amazed me. Time and time again, my question, "What are you doing?" would be answered with some version of, "You never said I couldn't do that!"

It wasn't much different when I worked with young adults or college-age students. All it did was take a different form. Instead of simply pushing the limit of the rules or subverting them, it was the never-ending methods they found to do foolish things. Really, it was impressive as I think back. Then again, you know what you are signing up for when you start working with these age groups. Plus, we have all been there. I have plenty of college stories to tell where, as I look back, I am rather amazed by my level of stupidity at times.

Regardless of the context, however, asking "What are you doing?" stemmed from the same issue—I didn't understand why something was happening and/or why someone was doing whatever they were doing. I had an expectation or belief regarding how things should go, and that person or event was not adhering to those expectations.

While I have been discussing this in a lighter sense, the question can certainly be asked in times and situations that are anything but funny and lighthearted. For many, this question gets asked during terribly difficult times. Whether it stems from abuse, betrayal, or other painful circumstances, the question, "What are you doing?" can be asked during the lowest or darkest moments of life.

The act of questioning itself is the common denominator in many situations that are strange, overwhelming, difficult, or disturbing. I have seen this happen repeatedly when people are faced with what they don't understand. Almost naturally, we question why we are going through whatever it is we are facing. We don't understand how or why we ended up in a terrible situation, so we instinctively question it.

Recall times in your life when you have gone through something difficult or unwanted. Was there not at least a moment where you questioned why it was happening? I find it hard to believe there is anyone who hasn't had questions cross their mind during those times. I certainly have not met that person. Once again, it seems questioning our circumstances when we don't want or understand them flows naturally as we experience them. And the hard truth is that the one we often pose those tough questions to during life's greatest adversities is God.

Questioning God

While I think questioning our circumstances is a common reaction for all humans, I also believe it is especially prevalent and, at times, problematic for Christians. Christians believe in an all-powerful God who is in control of all things. This would obviously include whatever situations we face. While that reality provides comfort and hope to many Christians as they walk through difficult times and seasons, it can also be rather disconcerting. If God is all-powerful, why is He allowing bad things to happen to His people? Why wouldn't He intervene? If He is good, wouldn't He want to stop the evil and pain that happens to His followers?

These questions and more flow from Christians as we are walking through tough times and difficult seasons. But since Christians believe in a personal God with whom we are able to have a relationship, we do more than think about these questions; we end up directing them to God Himself. We end up questioning God.

The reason we do this is that the questions that arise during these moments aren't just some academic exercise. No, instead, they are so often cries from the heart as we walk through difficulties, so why wouldn't we direct them toward the God who loves us? Why wouldn't we question the God who controls all things?

As we explore this idea of questioning God, I know there will be some people who bristle at the thought of this—mere humans questioning the God of the universe? We definitely shouldn't do that, right?

Well, there are countless examples of followers of God turning their gaze to the heavens and sending their questions up to God. It turns out there is a lot of precedent for it in the Bible, especially in the book of Psalms. Throughout the book, the reader sees example after example of the psalmist questioning God and lifting up his complaint to the almighty.

> Why, O LORD, do you stand far away? Why do you hide yourself in times of trouble?
>
> — Psalm 10:1

> [1] O God, why do you cast us off forever? Why does your anger smoke against the sheep of your pasture? [...] [10] How long, O God, is the foe to scoff? Is the enemy to revile your name forever? [11] Why do you hold back your hand, your right hand? Take it from the fold of your garment and destroy them!
>
> — Psalm 74:1, 10–11

> [7] Will the Lord spurn forever, and never again be favorable? [8] Has his steadfast love forever ceased? Are his promises at an end for all time? [9] Has God forgotten to be gracious? Has he in anger shut up his compassion?
>
> — Psalm 77:7–9

> [23] Awake! Why are you sleeping, O Lord?

> Rouse yourself! Do not reject us forever! [24] Why do you hide your face? Why do you forget our affliction and oppression? [25] For our soul is bowed down to the dust; our belly clings to the ground. [26] Rise up; come to our help! Redeem us for the sake of your steadfast love!
>
> — Psalm 44:23–26

These psalms and others like them contain powerful words. There is tremendous raw emotion and honesty within the psalmist's writings. There isn't some sort of pretense or holy veneer to what they say. Instead, there is honest struggle and questions that come pouring out before God. Once again, there seems to be something within us that reacts against what we are facing, and, as a result, we appeal to and question God.

But when we are talking about questioning God, we can't forget one of the most famous examples found in the Bible—the book of Job. The book records Job facing horrendous circumstances. He loses his family, possessions, and health. If that wasn't bad enough, after he loses all those things, Job's friends tell him that he must have done something wrong for all of this to happen. They figured there has to be a reason when bad stuff like this happens, and the reason appeared to be Job. Talk about adding insult to injury. It would be unbelievably devastating to lose what Job did, but if you add on "friends" blaming you as the reason it all happened, it seems hardly bearable.

Job wasn't going to take these indictments sitting down, though. He may not have been able to do anything about what he experienced, but he certainly wasn't going to accept the blame for it. Job was emphatic with his protests that he was innocent. He even starts to question God, asking, "Why have you made me your target? Have I become a burden to you?" (Job 7:20 NIV).

Job doesn't stop there, however. He eventually gets so worked up about protesting the notion of his guilt that he wants to plead his case to God directly. Job desires to set up a trial of sorts where he would get the chance to cross-examine God with different questions.

> [20] Only grant me two things, then I will not hide myself from your face: [21] withdraw your hand far from me, and let not dread of you terrify me. [22] Then call, and I will answer; or let me speak, and you reply to me. [23] How many are my iniquities and my sins? Make me know my transgression and my sin. [24] Why do you hide your face and count me as your enemy?
>
> —Job 13:20–24

The extent that Job was willing to go to question God and have his questions answered speaks to the extreme nature of what he was experiencing. Job's story, maybe more than any other, highlights the reality I hope has been clearly demonstrated by this point. When we are faced with tough situations or difficult circumstances, we instinctively have questions surrounding them, and as followers of God, we naturally want to direct those questions to the one who controls everything, God.

Why Habakkuk?

. . .

All of this leads us to the book of Habakkuk. If one was to summarize this book succinctly, I think an excellent way to do it would be to describe this book as one about questioning God. From the opening words of the dialogue, Habakkuk launches off into his questioning of God.

As I have highlighted, though, questioning God isn't unique, so what makes this book special? Well, I would answer that in two different ways. The first (and maybe most important) reason is God actually answers Habakkuk's questions, and God directly answering someone's questioning of Him was never guaranteed. A good example of this is once again found in Job. If you happen to not know how the book ends, God does appear to Job, but He doesn't answer Job's questions. Job never finds the answers he is seeking. With Habakkuk, however, God chooses to answer his questions.

Finally, I think the journey we as the readers embark on through Habakkuk's struggles as he questions God is extremely valuable. Where Habakkuk starts is completely different from where he ends. The progression teaches us a variety of lessons and almost welcomes us into the story because of its relatability.

All of this and so much more is what makes this book rather special. Really, it is noteworthy any time God provides insight into something as basic to the human experience as questioning our circumstances. But as we will see, there is so much more packed into this little, biblical book.

Also, don't think I will offer you mere philosophical and theological theories. The book of Habakkuk is also undoubtedly practical. It will provide us with tools that will assist us as we navigate through the situations and circumstances that cause us to question God. These tools will take different forms (e.g., lessons, a promise, and a timeless truth), but they are all incredibly valuable to us as we journey through this life. The relatability and applicability of the truths we explore in the coming pages make it a true gift from God to all of us.

A Prophet's Questions

> ¹ The oracle that Habakkuk the prophet saw. ² O LORD, how long shall I cry for help, and you will not hear? Or cry to you "Violence!" and you will not save? ³ Why do you make me see iniquity, and why do you idly look at wrong? Destruction and violence are before me; strife and contention arise. ⁴ So the law is paralyzed, and justice never goes forth. For the wicked surround the righteous; so justice goes forth perverted.
>
> — HABAKKUK 1:1–4

As we see, the book of Habakkuk wastes no time in revealing its main thrust—questioning God. The first words we have from Habakkuk are a question directed at God, and he doesn't stop there. Habakkuk rattles off other questions all centered around the same things. Habakkuk sees violence, injustice, and wickedness all around him.

God gave His people the law, which was the revealed way He wanted His people to live. However, that didn't seem to matter much because they disregarded it. What resulted was violence, destruction, conflicts, and suffering. When Habakkuk looked around, all he saw was God's will and way ignored and the injustice and suffering that resulted from it. Also, the righteous—the ones who were trying to follow God and His law—were suffering at the hands of the wicked.

If all that wasn't bad enough, the straw that seems to have broken the camel's back was God remained silent through all of this. Habakkuk sought God's help, but it appeared to the prophet that God didn't hear him. He called out to God about the violence and injustice, but God didn't do anything.

All of this moved Habakkuk to take the only action he could, which was to cry out more to God. Still, God didn't seem to be spurred to action despite evil abounding. God simply remained silent while the righteous suffered and evil ran rampant.

At the point where we find him in the book, Habakkuk can't take any more of this. It is too much for him; he is burdened and overwhelmed by everything that is going on. How can God continue to sit on the sidelines while all this is happening? How can God continue to ignore his prayers and the cries of the righteous? God needs to answer, so Habakkuk cries out again. But this time, he is questioning God.

Right from the beginning, I believe we see how relatable this book is. Who hasn't walked through something difficult and painful? If somehow you haven't, prepare yourself because it will eventually come. I say that not to be negative; it is simply a fact of life. If you are a Christian, Jesus said you will face trouble in this world (John 16:33). It is just an unfortunate result of sin. I don't care who you are or what your story is; you either have been through suffering and difficult situations, or you will in the future. This is our reality in the fallen and broken world we live in.

I am sure, like Habakkuk, as we walked through these times and situations, we would have loved to have answers about why we were experiencing what we were experiencing. I am sure we would have appreciated it if God had immediately intervened in our situations. During these times when we are calling out to God and seeking Him in the midst of our suffering and difficulties, like Habakkuk, I am also sure we have wondered why God seems silent. Really, how can anyone not feel this way?

If you ever felt bad for having these feelings, just look at Habakkuk. It is important to remember that Habakkuk was a prophet of God, so he had a unique relationship with Him. Habakkuk certainly knew God and interacted with Him in a rather special way. Despite this fact, however, Habakkuk still questioned God in the middle of his struggles. He still cried out, wondering where God was.

This is why I said we need to simply look at Habakkuk. I believe the record of a prophet questioning God should encourage every other follower of God. Even if you find yourself in a place where you feel you have no other recourse other than crying out to God and questioning Him, you are in good company. You'd be in the company of this prophet and others such as the great king and psalmist David.

Lament

I have said it over and over again, but it bears repeating. Bringing our complaints to God in the form of questioning Him seems to flow from us naturally as we experience and walk through difficult things. Why then is there so much stigma around it, and why do so many Christians spurn the idea of expressing our pain and difficulties?

I think one of the reasons has something to do with what has crept into Christianity over the years. It is the idea that, when faced with difficult situations or terrible circumstances, Christians need to simply "buck up." It has gotten to the point where many Christians I talk to are convinced they should never feel down. It doesn't matter the situation and how difficult it may be; they believe they just need to pick themselves up and stop letting it affect them. While I agree in one sense that Christians should be some of the happiest people (see Jonathan Edward's sermon titled "Christian Happiness"), that still doesn't mean we are all somehow immune to the pain that can come from walking through this life.

Another reason Christians don't feel at liberty to be honest about their feelings is due to the "health and wealth" version of Christianity that has continued to deceive many. It convinces Christians that, if they are going through something negative like sickness, pain, or really almost any bad situation, all they need to do is just have more faith. According to those who affirm such beliefs, the reason having more faith is the key is because God's will for His followers is to be happy, healthy, and blessed. If we aren't happy, healthy, and blessed, those who adhere to this view posit there must be something wrong with us and our faith in God because He is always looking to pour out blessing after blessing! Unfortunately, not only does this not represent a biblical view of this world (e.g., John 16:33), but it leaves subscribers to this viewpoint without the tools to navigate through those difficult times that will inevitably come their way.

Regardless of the form it takes, many Christians are convinced they cannot let themselves be affected by what this life might throw at them. Christians apparently always need to have a stiff upper lip.

Now, I don't think Christians who espouse these views are necessarily conniving to be hurtful or lead other Christians astray (prosperity gospel preachers and proponents aside). I think most Christians are trying to be helpful. However, it not only doesn't accomplish that purpose, but it also loses sight of one of the most prevalent types of writing in the Bible—laments.

If you don't know, laments are ways that people mourn and express deep sorrow, sadness, and/or pain. Laments are found throughout the Bible, with an entire book of the Bible being devoted to the act of lamenting (Lamentations). Much of the psalms contain what most people think of when they think about a biblical lament. Over a third of the psalms either are or contain laments.

Laments can take different forms throughout the pages of Scripture, but for our purposes, questioning God can also be a form of lament. If you were to look back at the psalms I included previously or the example from Job, these individuals are expressing their pain and sadness, and their lament takes the form of questioning God.

Even though their prominence throughout Scripture should make it apparent how important laments are, Christians today seem to have lost our understanding of them and their significance. Instead of joining many of the biblical greats and the scores of other followers of God throughout the ages who have used laments to express their plight before God and man, contemporary Christians choose to pass on this and instead adopt some sort of stoicism, often under the guise that this is how God wants us to act.

Here is the reality, however: God is a big God. Not only does He know what we are going through, but He also knows how difficult it can be for us to walk through whatever life throws at us. As a matter of fact, through Jesus, God sympathizes with the difficulties we face and the weaknesses we have (Heb. 4:15). So, God does not mind whenever we call out to Him in our pain and suffering. I would even go so far as to say that He welcomes it. What parent wouldn't want their children to come to him or her when they are hurting or going through difficulties? Even during times when the pain is raw and we want to lash out, there is still grace for us from a loving God who understands our frailty.

Jesus Wept

One of my favorite biblical stories is one that I believe demonstrates how God's heart is moved by our pain—when Jesus raised Lazarus from the dead. When Jesus arrived at the place where Lazarus was buried, He knew He was going to raise His friend from the dead. Still, he wept (John 11:35). Why? He was moved by the pain and brokenness death had caused.

When Mary vented her frustration to Him regarding His absence and the role that played in Lazarus' death, Jesus didn't scold Mary. No, instead there were tears. The heart of God was moved by the brokenness sin had caused as demonstrated in Lazarus' death. And I believe when we go to God in our pain and suffering—even though it may be crude and far from what the God of the universe should receive—His heart is still moved because of His love for us.

Why am I saying all of this? It's simple. No one should ever feel they can't or shouldn't go to God with their struggles and difficulties, even if they come in the form of questioning Him. Our God loves us, so as we experience these things, we have to know God is there for us even in our act of asking Him tough questions.

This is what I love about the beginning of Habakkuk's book. It starts with a follower of God questioning Him. It doesn't waste any time; it simply jumps into the heart of the matter. Habakkuk is struggling, and he is looking for answers.

What is Habakkuk struggling with, though? We know he is going through something that caused him to question God, but what exactly is Habakkuk experiencing that got him to that point? There are two central aspects to Habakkuk's complaint against God.

Unanswered Prayer

The question Habakkuk leads with is, "How long ... must I call for help, but you do not listen" (1:2 NIV). Habakkuk is crying out to God, but God is eerily silent. Honestly, this has to be one of the most frustrating things when it comes to following God, and it is something I believe leads us to question Him more than maybe anything else.

Prayer is the language of how we approach the eternal God. It is or should be the lifeblood of every believer. Nowhere is this exemplified to a greater degree than when Paul instructs his readers to pray without ceasing (1 Thess. 5:17). So, if we are praying and seeking God—doing everything we can and using the mechanism He gave us to bring our requests and burdens before Him—without Him answering, frustration is almost inevitable.

If you were to go back and look again at the psalms I referenced earlier, all of them had an aspect of questioning God due to His perceived silence. The psalmist in Psalm 44 described his feelings by declaring that God was sleeping, and the psalmist wouldn't be alone in having such feelings. What Christian hasn't wondered why God wasn't answering his or her prayers? I would even go as far as to suggest that, during the times when we are praying and seeking God continuously for things, we would rather get an answer that doesn't go the way we want instead of not getting an answer at all! There is just this terrible, lingering state we fall into when God doesn't answer. We know that God hears us, but it feels as though He doesn't.

For Habakkuk, even though he was crying out for help, he felt as though God wasn't listening. In his sorrow, he raises his requests to God, but all he receives in return is silence.

Lack of Intervention

Building on the first aspect of his complaint which was unanswered prayer, there is another concern on the prophet's heart. It isn't just that God isn't answering his prayer; it is also God refusing to intervene in what would appear to be something that should move God to want to intervene. It is one thing if God doesn't answer your prayers, but it is something else entirely for evil, sin, and injustice to be running rampant while God seems to remain aloof.

Isn't this one of the most common objections to God and His existence? Specifically, evil is one of the greatest and most powerful counterarguments against God. Sure, there are plenty of academic answers regarding how evil and God can coexist and why God allows it to happen, but that does nothing for the emotional and spiritual toll that evil takes on an individual or a community.

If God is good and loving, how can He sit on the sidelines while these things are going on? How can He remain silent and allow things that are against His will and His ways to continue? Even worse, so many times it seems those who don't strive to follow God and His ways succeed more than the ones who do!

Habakkuk sees injustice and wickedness all around, and he is crying out to God regarding it. But God, according to Habakkuk, watches and sits idly by. Also, to add to the difficulty of this situation for Habakkuk, it is God's own people who are carrying out the evil and corruption. If all this still wasn't bad enough, it also seems as though someone in Habakkuk's day would be better off not following God's will and way rather than following it.

For Habakkuk, it just doesn't make sense why God wouldn't step into the situation and save His people. It doesn't make sense why God wouldn't intervene to correct the way everything is playing out. How can God let His people who are called by His name (2 Chron. 7:14) experience such injustice?

This is what led Habakkuk to question God. God's silence and seeming refusal to intervene and answer prayers have pushed Habakkuk to the point where he can take no more.

In highlighting these aspects of Habakkuk's complaint against God, I think the same concerns are often at the heart of why we question Him. Each of these aspects can put us right where Habakkuk found himself—wanting answers from God.

That is why Habakkuk's story probably sounds extremely familiar to many. Maybe it is unanswered prayers or a lack of intervention. Maybe we don't understand why something is happening or why God is doing what He is doing. Maybe we had expectations and beliefs regarding how things should go, but there isn't anything adhering to those expectations. Maybe it is something else.

Really, if we could simplify this first part by boiling everything down to its essence, I believe there is a question that encapsulates not only Habakkuk's questions but also ours—"What are you doing, God?"

I think Habakkuk's questions and complaint could be easily combined into this one question. That is why I gave the book this title. I think it is the question we all have for God when we are frustrated and struggling.

As you continue through the rest of the book, keep this in

mind—there is a progression to Habakkuk's story. At the beginning, the lessons we draw from the narrative may seem simple or well-known if you have been a Christian for any amount of time, but don't stop! Not only are those lessons valuable tools for us as we navigate through difficult times in our lives, but they also provide the foundation for the deeper truths that come later in the book.

You'll never fully understand the beautiful message that Habakkuk's book is trying to communicate if you don't take each step in the journey. If it seems basic at first, don't worry; there is a lot more in store as you progress through the story. But also, don't overlook the lessons even if they seem familiar. Sometimes, there is importance in the familiar. Don't miss out on what God could be speaking to you simply because you think you already understand a lesson.

Through the pain Habakkuk felt due to the brokenness all around him, God has something important to say to Habakkuk. Ultimately, I believe that what God will reveal in this biblical book will go on to be incredibly useful to Habakkuk and anyone else who finds themselves wanting to question God.

2
DIRECTIVE

One of the churches I worked at previously was a very large church that had plenty of big-name speakers come through. Whether it was for conferences or other engagements, there was a proverbial "who's who" of Christian speakers making stops at the church. From time to time, I would get the opportunity to chat with these speakers. While the context in which I would talk to the speakers varied (maybe in a formal setting or maybe while I hosted him or her), I always viewed it as a great opportunity to learn something. They all had their own stories of how they got to the unique place in which they found themselves, so for someone who was young and new in ministry, I reveled in the chance to glean something from each person.

One of my go-to moves when I finally had my chance to talk with these individuals was to ask them one very specific question. My goal was always to ask many different questions, but I wanted to make sure I at least asked this one question if that's all I could manage. By asking this question to all these different people, I was able to compare and contrast the answers while also exploring the unique way each one answered it.

Now, I learned a lot by doing this. The answers these men and women of God gave were often enlightening and always helpful. But I learned something else as I continued this practice. If all I did was take in the answer, I would have missed some important lessons buried within their response. Sure, the answer itself was obviously important, but there were always some other great lessons that only came from looking a little deeper.

For instance, I had one speaker explain to me an important part of his journey that helped shape him. As he was explaining, I found it full of very helpful information, but as I started thinking about it more after he left, I saw there were other truths I could draw from his story. There were aspects of it that he may not have specifically highlighted, but I could see the immense value right below the surface.

I have tried to continue this practice even now when I talk to people. As I ask questions and attempt to learn things from others, I want to pay careful attention to not only what is said but how and why it is said. I do this because I am convinced there is always a valuable lesson or truth to be had if we dig just a little deeper for it.

It may come as no surprise that this practice I used with speakers has shaped how I interact with a variety of different things, including Scripture. And when I read the book of Habakkuk, I can't help but think back to the questions I asked and all lessons I learned from the different speakers.

As we saw in the last chapter, Habakkuk asks God some pretty biting questions. Now, as we read on, we see something rather incredible—God shows up to answer Habakkuk's questions. Any time God appears and speaks is meaningful, but His response to Habakkuk is particularly noteworthy. As a way of reminder, here are Habakkuk's questions:

> ² O LORD, how long shall I cry for help, and you will not hear? Or cry to you "Violence!" and you will not save? ³ Why do you make me see iniquity, and why do you idly look at wrong?
>
> — HABAKKUK 1:2–3

Why does it seem like I cry out, and you don't hear? Why won't you intervene and save us against evil? Why do you just sit by and watch wrong happen? Those certainly are tough questions, but as I mentioned, God will address them. Look at how God starts His response:

> Look among the nations, and see; wonder and be astounded. For I am doing a work in your days that you would not believe if told.
>
> — HABAKKUK 1:5

I think it is quite interesting that this is how God starts His response. God doesn't immediately give Habakkuk His plan regarding how He will deal with the injustice and wickedness that burdened him. Instead, God starts His response by giving Habakkuk a directive and then a promise.

Even though Habakkuk wasn't looking for those things, the directive and promise are just as important to God's response as His plan because of what God is teaching Habakkuk through them. Every part of the response God gives to Habakkuk has important lessons tied to it that Habakkuk and, subsequently, his readers will benefit from hearing. In this chapter, we will focus on the first thing God gives to Habakkuk—a directive.

· · ·

The Directive

> Look among the nations, and see; wonder and be astounded. ...
>
> — HABAKKUK 1:5

God starts His response to Habakkuk by directing him to look around. God wants him to notice the other nations and see something. But what exactly does God want Habakkuk to see? Though we aren't looking at the promise in this chapter, it is impossible to fully separate these two and still understand what God is communicating. So, God's directive for Habakkuk is fully revealed when we examine all of verse five together. Again, God's instruction to Habakkuk was to "look among the nations, and see; wonder and be astounded. ..."

> For I am doing a work in your days that you would not believe if told.
>
> — HABAKKUK 1:5

God wants Habakkuk to see that He is doing a work. This seems like a rather peculiar way to start an answer to the serious complaint brought to Him by His prophet, but through this directive and promise, God is actually addressing Habakkuk's concerns directly.

With this in mind, starting His response with a directive that focuses on what Habakkuk was seeing is rather ingenious. The reason it is so smart is that a major part of Habakkuk's complaint revolved around what he was seeing—injustice and wickedness. This is why God begins His answer with a clever directive. And through this directive, God brings light to an issue Habakkuk and all of us have when we are in similar positions.

When we are surrounded by things we don't want or understand, our gaze so often begins to narrow. Our focus starts to become limited to what we are experiencing or what is happening around us. We can lose sight of anything beyond the immediate horizon of our circumstances.

While this should almost be an expected response to bad things happening in our lives, it is often not a positive one. When we narrow our focus, we can become blinded to other realities or even completely lose touch with anything else going on around us or in our world.

To illustrate, take the topic of persecution within Christianity. This is a topic that seems to come up more and more in American Christianity. As our culture slides further and further from its bedrock of Judeo-Christian values, cries of persecution ring out from scores of Christians.

Now, even though there has undoubtedly been more pushback and rejection of Christians and our deeply held values and beliefs, should this be considered persecution? If one only had the perspective of recent history within a place like the United States, it would seem that way.

However, anyone who has understands Church history or what is happening to Christians in other parts of the world would know that Christians in America are hardly facing persecution in any comparative sense. Sure, things may not be what they were and seem to be progressing more and more in an undesirable direction, but what we are facing in America as I write this hardly qualifies as persecution when you compare it to what other Christians are experiencing.

One of the events I think provides a humorous example of this is the annual complaint regarding the war on Christmas. Year after year, so many Christians work themselves into an outrage regarding what is viewed as a war raging around the Christmas holiday. There are always pronouncements concerning the continued erosion of the meaning of the holiday and how it is a sign of the growing persecution Christians are facing here in America. Since Christmas isn't recognized or celebrated the way many Christians are accustomed to, the conclusion is that it must be a sign of growing persecution.

My favorite harbinger of this apparent growing persecution has been the uproar over what is on the Starbucks cups during the holiday season. For years now, the Starbucks cup has become the front line where the battle over values and traditions is ostensibly fought between Christians and the secular world.

I am obviously having some fun with this, but it is an issue for many people and has been for years. Pages have been written covering the "War on Christmas" with the Starbucks holiday cup front and center.

Instead of being a sign of persecution, though, I think this actually shows how blessed we are as Christians in America, where this would even be considered anything other than a private business' choice of what to do with their cups. If a cup from Starbucks is one of the biggest signs of persecution that Christians face in this country, I would say we are extremely fortunate. Putting aside the fact that there are countries who do not observe Christmas as a public holiday, there are Christians all over the world who would love to have the problems we complain about and would gladly trade them for the ones they are having.

Recently, I read a report detailing six months of Christian

persecution from around the world, and the story contained examples of Christians being beaten, lynched, sodomized, and killed (twenty Christians were killed in one instance while simply attending a wedding), among other things. Another report from a different part of the world highlighted how Christian families from some areas are now under constant surveillance, with officials waiting for them to make mistakes so they can exact harsh punishments. This means they can't even go out for a family day without the government intervening one way or another in their affairs. Yet again, a report from a different area highlighted Christians from a specific region being taken from their homes or places of worship. One pastor was brutally murdered because he wouldn't capitulate to his captors' demands over his faith.

I am sure Christians in these areas wish one of the greatest acts of persecution against their faith was a coffee cup design or whether or not other people say "Merry Christmas" instead of "Happy Holidays."

Honestly, this is why I read and try to communicate to my church what is happening to Christians in other parts of the world. We can easily become so focused on what is happening to us and in our immediate frame of reference that we lose sight of the bigger picture. Or worse, we can begin to think what we are seeing and experiencing is just the norm or representative of what is happening elsewhere.

Though Habakkuk's complaint was far more serious than a coffee cup design, he had fallen into the same trap. Habakkuk questioned God regarding why He wasn't intervening, but through His directive, God responded by pointing out that Habakkuk's focus and perspective were far too narrow. If Habakkuk simply looked outside of his experience and surroundings, he may have seen something different. Really, if

Habakkuk had the right perspective, he would have understood he had no ground to stand on regarding his complaint against God. Sure, things were not going how he wanted in his limited sphere, but that didn't mean God was not acting in other ways or places. The prophet needed a change of perspective.

Change Your Perspective

This is the lesson we can all learn from God's directive. When we are in a place where we are questioning God, we need to practice changing our perspective. A broader perspective may be needed and extremely helpful during those times when we run into difficulties. It is so easy for our circumstances to consume us, and when they do, we can lose sight of how our current experience fits into the broader context. By moving our perspective off of ourselves and our immediate sphere, we begin to gain a better understanding of what is really happening.

Now, apply this lesson to the example levied above regarding Christian persecution. One can become so consumed with the idea of American Christians being persecuted that even a coffee cup is a harbinger of this reality. But in light of what has happened and is happening to so many Christians in other parts of the world, what a company like Starbucks does with their coffee cup is patently unimportant and certainly nowhere near anything that could be considered persecution. It isn't until those who hold this view change their perspective that they can begin to see more of the greater picture.

In order to understand the importance of this lesson, one doesn't need to only focus on a negative example like the one I used above concerning persecution. It can also help Christians see positive things that are unfolding when it appears there isn't much around them that could be considered positive.

Another complaint I often hear from American Christians (and really Christians all across different Western cultures) is the fact that religion is falling out of favor. There is much bemoaning among Christians and celebrating among the irreligious regarding the decline of religion, including Christianity. While this decline may be true in America and other places in the West, it certainly isn't true in other areas of the world. As a matter of fact, different religions are growing almost everywhere else. This means that, with a change in perspective, the person who is saddened by the decline of religion could instead feel encouraged due to various religions growing in so many other places.

In a way, this is what God is trying to get Habakkuk to understand. God wants him to look around and see something else besides what he has been focusing on. Sure, things may not be going particularly great around him at the moment, but that isn't all there is. Really, Habakkuk needs to remember that God is not just some tribal deity like many of the gods of the nations around Judah. God is the God of the universe. He is over all things and working all things out according to His plan. This includes everything Habakkuk is seeing and experiencing. It also includes everything happening in all other nations.

Habakkuk's complaint and questions were centered around his nation and his experience, but God is not limited to one nation. Once again, God is at work across all nations and with all people. So right from the beginning of His response, God challenges Habakkuk to expand his narrow focus and change his perspective. God does this because He knows a change of perspective is necessary at times to help us move beyond ourselves and see the greater picture.

If you look at verse five as a whole, including the second part of the verse after the directive, I believe God is not only telling Habakkuk that his perspective needs to change, but He goes so far as to suggest that if Habakkuk had this different perspective (where he was looking around and seeing what God was really up to), Habakkuk would be astounded. His reaction would be wonder rather than despair.

The bottom line is this—God is at work. Whether Habakkuk or anyone else is looking for it or can grasp it, God is doing something.

What is Habakkuk complaining about then? Habakkuk has been complaining and questioning God because it doesn't appear to him that God is doing anything, but the first part of God's response is to point out that Habakkuk is wrong.

The issue isn't that God is inactive—Habakkuk just isn't seeing it. Sure, God may not be doing what Habakkuk wants or working in the ways he thinks God should be, but that doesn't mean God is silent, not working, or not answering prayers. He is doing something not only in Judah but all around Habakkuk. As a matter of fact, as He continues His response, God will show Habakkuk that not only is He working, but He is also working in the very things that caused Habakkuk to question Him in the first place. Maybe it is difficult to see, but if Habakkuk changed his perspective from beyond what he was experiencing, he might not have questioned God in the first place.

What Are We Looking at?

For us, the lesson is similar. If we find ourselves surrounded by wickedness and evil ... if it seems like there is injustice all around us ... if we are faced with tremendous difficulty or pain, let's heed God's directive. Whatever it is we are experiencing or facing that causes us to question God, let's look at Habakkuk's story and take seriously the lesson that instructs us to change our perspective. We need to do what God says by looking around and seeing things outside of our situations and immediate surroundings.

I want to offer a final suggestion as this chapter closes. There are many ways to apply this lesson, but one thing I do that I am convinced assists us with changing our perspective is to go out and experience God's creation.

In our world, we are always on the go. For most people, a day is filled with work, family time, housework, hobbies, and much more. The days and weeks can fly by without us even noticing. With that in mind, I think there is something helpful in slowing down, going out in creation, and taking time to revel in it. There is something special about being out in God's creation that can not only be calming and therapeutic but can also help us refocus and gain a proper perspective.

How can anyone go out at night, look up at the stars, and not have their perspective readjusted? I find there is nothing that can help with my focus and perspective more than looking up at the night sky and thinking about the vastness of space. We are so small and insignificant in comparison to what we are looking at, but God still loved us enough to make a way for us to have a relationship with Him.

Since the heavens declare God's glory, and the sky declares His handiwork (Ps. 19:1), the incredible vista above with countless stars also reminds us of the power and greatness of our God. In Isaiah, God, through the author, challenged those who would be reading to also look at the sky and be amazed at what it says about Him:

> [25] To whom then will you compare me, that I
> should be like him? says the Holy One. [26]

> Lift up your eyes on high and see: who created these? He who brings out their host by number, calling them all by name; by the greatness of his might and because he is strong in power, not one is missing.
>
> — Isaiah 40:25–26

Interestingly, God is doing the same thing in Isaiah that He does in Habakkuk. He is directing His audience to look and see what is already around them. In Habakkuk, it was regarding the other nations and what God was doing there. In Isaiah, it is also about what God was doing, but it was far beyond just other nations. It was everything in the heavens above.

You see, God knows we lose sight of the bigger picture. He knows what we are seeing or experiencing will become our focal point. That is why God is directing Habakkuk, Isaiah's readers, and all of us through His response to look around—to change our perspective!

I am not saying this shift will be easy. There are many times when it is tough or seems impossible, but if we find ourselves at the place where we are questioning God, it's a directive and lesson we have to follow. I am also not suggesting that changing our perspective will answer all our questions or immediately alleviate our concerns. No, instead, what I am saying is the change of perspective can strengthen us to keep following God even through the toughest times.

Maybe, like Habakkuk, we can't see what God is up to in what we are experiencing. But whether we see it or not, through this lesson, we can always remember that God is working out His plan and purpose in the world. If God is great enough to know the stars by name and caring enough to make sure birds get fed (Matt. 6:26), we can know He is great enough to care for us also.

So even now, know that God is working in whatever situation and place we find ourselves. And during the times when we lose sight of this and God's greatness, let us once again heed the directive He gave to Habakkuk and apply its lesson to our lives.

3
PROMISE

One thing that has appeared in my personality over the years is that I really gained a love of learning. Whether it is picking the brains of church speakers or just generally absorbing as much information as I can, I somehow turned into a learner. If you asked my parents if I had a love for learning as a kid, I'm not sure you would have been met with a positive response. I always found ways to get good enough grades, but I just did what I had to do to get by.

It wasn't until I started working on my first graduate degree that I began to realize how much I loved learning new things. I am not sure if I just matured into it or if there is some other reason that it blossomed, but it is something I now enjoy.

This love of learning has served me well as I stepped into a position where I preach every week. While there are pastors (some I know) who look at their sermon preparation as simply something you check off during the week, I love sitting down and seeing what I can teach. To be clear, there certainly are times when it is laborious and tiresome, but I get so energized when I discover something that ministers to me because I know I get to teach it to my congregation.

One recent sermon series I preached covered the promises of God. Teaching on the promises of God isn't something new or groundbreaking. Some of the most popular and well-known verses in all of the Bible are God's promises. But as I started down the path of studying for the series, I was blown away by what I was learning.

I thought narrowing down the list of promises would be a pretty easy task, but that ended up not being the case. I am not sure how many promises God gave, but they all seemed to be ministering to me in new and powerful ways. I felt as though I was discovering many of the promises all over again for the first time.

This was exactly what happened when I read the promise that God gave to Habakkuk. Though I read the book many times previously, I was taken aback by God's promise and how powerful it is. All I could think was, "Why haven't I heard more sermons or teachings covering this promise?" Though I am not sure why that is the case, I think this promise deserves the spotlight.

God's Promise to Habakkuk

The last chapter highlighted the beginning of God's response to Habakkuk's questions and complaint. We looked at the first part of verse five that contained the directive God gave to Habakkuk. Now, let's dive into the second half of the verse, which contains the promise.

> Look among the nations, and see; wonder and
>   be astounded. For I am doing a work in your
>   days that you would not believe if told.

— HABAKKUK 1:5

Remember, God wants Habakkuk to look outside of himself, his immediate situation, and his surroundings in order to see something. What is Habakkuk supposed to be seeing, though? God makes it clear with His promise—He is working in Habakkuk's day.

Just as it is difficult to understand why God seems to be silent or inactive in our situations, it also difficult for Christians to grasp what God is doing even if we know He is working. When you're in the middle of a tough time, it can be hard, if not impossible, to see how God is working through your situation. However, the story of countless people is that, after they were able to look back on what they went through, they could see God was working in everything they were facing.

That is always a great thing to hear, but it leads to the question: Why aren't we able to see God's work and plan unfolding when we're in the midst of our difficulties? Why is it so hard to see God's hand at work during those times?

Certainly, as we talked about in the last chapter, our focus tightens, and we need to change our perspective if we are going to see what God is doing. While this is true, there is another reason why I believe it is so hard at times for us to recognize God is at work in our difficulties. That is because we assume, if God were doing something, things would be going differently, or we would see our circumstances changing.

If you look back at Habakkuk's complaint, you get the sense this had to have crossed his mind. Look again at what he says to God:

> ³ Why do you make me see iniquity, and why do you idly look at wrong? Destruction and

> violence are before me; strife and
> contention arise. ⁴ So the law is paralyzed,
> and justice never goes forth. For the wicked
> surround the righteous; so justice goes forth
> perverted.
>
> — HABAKKUK 1:3–4

For Habakkuk, it doesn't make sense how God can see all of the wrongs that are transpiring and sit idly by. He knows everything that is happening doesn't line up with who God is and His character. This is why he is struggling to understand why God appears to not care enough to act on the situation—why He remains idle.

The key, though, is that it doesn't *appear* God is working. How does Habakkuk arrive at the conclusion that God is not working and is sitting idly by? Well, he seems to assume that if God was at work in what he was seeing and experiencing, then things wouldn't be going the way they were.

You see, Habakkuk's line of reasoning is something that can happen to us all. I think it is important to point out how prevalent this is when it comes to God operating in the world. So many of our questions directed at God are centered around these types of thoughts. Time and time again, we are not only confused as to why God appears to not be working in the situations we are facing, but we are convinced, if He would just intervene, things would go differently.

What it all boils down to for Habakkuk and us (if we hold these thoughts) is we simply can't wrap our minds around what God is doing (or not doing) in the circumstances we face. In Habakkuk's situation, he couldn't reconcile how an all-powerful, good God could be actively working in what he was seeing and experiencing, considering injustice and wickedness were running rampant. It is as if Habakkuk is saying through his complaint, "All of this doesn't make sense to me!"

The first thing God communicated in His response to Habakkuk was the need to change his perspective. That was the lesson from the directive. Now, through the promise, we see another lesson Habakkuk and everyone who finds themselves questioning God needs to put into practice—accepting our limitations.

Accept Our Limitations

Through His response, God is telling Habakkuk and anyone else who would question Him that we can't even scratch the surface in trying to understand Him. We can't hope to genuinely grasp all He is doing in our situations. His ways truly are higher than our ways, and His thoughts are higher than our thoughts (Isa. 55:8–9). So it is foolish to assume we can even begin to fathom all God is doing in the world.

What we are left with in light of this reality is the lesson that we have to accept our limitations when it comes to trying to understand God and how He is working. This is especially true when it deals with how He is working in our lives and circumstances.

Even if we took the first lesson to heart and changed our perspective, we can still be left in a place where we are questioning God. A major reason for this is, even when we can see Him working everywhere else, we are often left wondering why He doesn't seem to be working in what we are experiencing. It is a tough reality, but one experienced by many.

However, the problem isn't with God. He is working, and almost all Christians accept that reality, even if it is just generally. Really, the problem we all run into lies in the fact that we can't possibly hope to always understand what God is up to. Again, the problem isn't really that God isn't working; the problem is we can't grasp everything (or at times anything) God is doing.

This means changing our perspective isn't enough. For most people, a perspective change alone won't assuage their questions and complaints. We also have to come to grips with the reality of how limited we are in our understanding of God and how He works in our lives and in the world.

Now, I know there will be some who find that idea discouraging. If we are questioning God, we are obviously struggling, so this reality doesn't seem to inspire much hope.

I actually think that shouldn't be the case, though. I believe this reality, when properly understood, should do the exact opposite. It should give us even more hope. It is what makes the promise given to Habakkuk so encouraging to anyone facing difficult times or circumstances.

In order to explain why I believe this, look at a well-known and oft-quoted promise Paul pens many years later. The reason this beloved promise has given so many Christians hope is the same reason God's promise to Habakkuk should also spur hope.

> And we know that in all things God works for
> the good of those who love him, who have
> been called according to his purpose.
>
> — Romans 8:28 (NIV)

Paul tells his readers that God is working in all things. Regardless of the situation and no matter how terrible it is, God is still at work in it. Paul doesn't stop there, however. He goes on to explain that not only is God working in each and every situation, but the way He is working in that situation will eventually result in our good and God's glory. Regardless of what is happening or what we may be seeing and experiencing, God is in such control of every aspect that we can be absolutely sure the outcome will be a good one for all who follow God.

In a way, Paul is bringing out the same reality God was communicating in His promise to Habakkuk. God communicates it in a decidedly different way, but the general truth remains—God is in control and working in all things regardless of the circumstances. What is important isn't just that God is working in each and every situation we face, though. Also, just as important is how He is working in those situations. Once again, He is working in such a way that the ultimate result will be for our good and His glory.

As I talk about what is important, you will notice something doesn't come up in the discussion, and that is our understanding of what God is doing. This is because it's not at all consequential that we fully understand everything surrounding what God is doing and why He is doing it. This is why God ends the promise He gave Habakkuk with the statement that Habakkuk "would not believe" even if he was told what God was doing.

Think about it. Habakkuk couldn't grasp it even if he wanted to. Everything regarding what, why, and how God is doing His work is so far beyond Habakkuk and us. God in His infinite wisdom knows we can't understand all the details. So, what does God do? He leaves us with these promises and the reality that is demonstrated over and over again in Scripture—God is in control and working it all out for our good and His glory.

We cannot remain in the trap so many of us fall into where, just because we can't see it or understand it, we find ourselves frustrated or questioning God. Even if it is such a dark time where it seems almost impossible God could be working in it,

He is there. God is always working in and through whatever it is we are facing or experiencing.

This is the beauty and power of the promise God gives to Habakkuk. All Habakkuk could see was injustice and wickedness around him. He saw the righteous being overrun by the wicked. It was so burdensome to him, but it didn't seem like God cared enough to answer his prayers or intervene.

The promise of God for Habakkuk, however, is that He is doing a work even in the midst of all Habakkuk was seeing and experiencing. Also, the work God is doing is so great that Habakkuk wouldn't even believe it if he was told.

Again, I want to draw your attention to that sentiment because it is why I love this promise. God is working in such a way in Habakkuk's situation and surroundings that it would leave him dumbfounded if he found out. And as we will eventually see, it is absolutely true!

Wouldn't Believe If Told

Think about how this applies to the contemporary world. As I write this, the country is struggling with a pandemic, and it has affected many people in a variety of ways. As a pastor, I have seen what this time has done to people, and it can be heartbreaking. In addition, I am also continuously grieved by what I am seeing transpire in our culture. Rampant injustices, loss of civility, cultural divides, and a general yet extreme decline in morality that borders on wickedness highlight just a few of the cultural issues swirling around.

If that wasn't enough, it is hard to look at the state of so many Christians and churches without becoming dismayed. While there is certainly increased opposition to Christianity and its institutions, what I find most disheartening are wounds that seem self-inflicted. In a time when the light of Christ can and should be shining so brightly in this country, Christians cannot stop the infighting enough to be a light to those around them. Whether it is arguments about the pandemic, politics, or other social issues, Christians can't seem to resist attacking their own brothers and sisters in Christ long enough to see the damage they are doing and the opportunity we are missing to be a source of healing and unity.

I believe many of us find ourselves exactly where Habakkuk found himself—surrounded and almost disillusioned by the injustice and wickedness all around. It seems as though no one can escape the constant barrage of bad news and despondency. All of this and more is truly enough to make one throw their hands up to the heavens and scream out the questions, "Why aren't you intervening? Why are you just sitting idly by? Why aren't you answering our prayers? What are you doing, God?!"

And while I believe anyone who finds themselves in this place would be justified, I also believe God's response would be the same for us as it was for Habakkuk:

> I am doing a work in your days that you would
> not believe if told.
>
> — HABAKKUK 1:5

God is at work. That was God's promise for Habakkuk, and His promise still stands today. He is at work in any and every situation, whether we can see or understand it. So while the promise was given to a specific person in a specific place at a specific time, the testimony of Scripture reveals the promise is just as applicable to us.

If we had even an inkling of what God was up to in our lives and the world around us, I know we would be blown away. If we had even the slightest clue of what His plans were for us and our situations, we wouldn't believe it.

This means that regardless of how much you have messed up, how many terrible things have happened to you, how much your life and the world around you seem to be falling apart, God is still working in it. And if He told you what He was doing and what He would accomplish through it, you wouldn't trust the answer because it wouldn't make sense to you. That is how great our God is!

This is why I have grown to love this promise so much. It is a reminder that not only is God always working in our lives and everything we are seeing and experiencing, but it also brings us back to this reality—whatever God is up to would be mind-blowing if we found out!

Sure, things may still be extremely difficult. If we are questioning God, they most certainly are in one way or another. But this promise should give every follower of God an overflow of hope. As you're looking right in the face of sickness, pain, brokenness, shattered relationships, death, or whatever else shakes us to our core, we have this promise that reassures us that somehow—whether we ever understand it or see it—God is working in and through it all in such a way where we wouldn't even believe it if we were told. It will all work out for our good and His ultimate glory. This is a place where we can draw our strength during those difficult times.

Also, this is why I previously said the idea that we can never expect to fully understand what God is up to in the world or in our lives should still result in hope. Yes, it is frustrating when we can't wrap our minds around why things are happening, but we still have this promise that tells us God is working. And we know if God is working, we can be sure the result will be a good one.

All of this and more is why this promise has become so meaningful to me. I think it is severely underrated as far as biblical promises go. Also, since I believe in the importance and power of the promise, I think the lesson we derive from it is just as important. The lesson that we need to accept our limitations becomes a way the promise manifests itself practically in our lives. If we don't learn to accept our limitations, how can we ever have peace and be able to trust God in the middle of life's darkest valleys? We will be continually riddled with fear, worry, and uncertainty when we don't have to be. We will spend unnecessary amounts of time trying to figure things out when there is a very real chance we may never understand why it is happening to us.

On the other side of the coin, however, if we do accept our limitations—if we recognize that we will always be limited in our understanding of God and what He is up to—then we can move forward through the dark times knowing and trusting that God is working it all out for our good and His glory. We won't spend our time worrying or trying to work out all the details because we will have already settled in our hearts this lesson regarding our limitations. Instead, we can rest by casting our anxieties, burdens, and questions onto God, knowing He cares for us (1 Pet. 5:7).

I want to put forward an example I think demonstrates this reality beautifully. It is the story of Elizabeth Elliot. Elizabeth, her husband Jim, and other missionaries moved into an area near a tribe in Ecuador that they hoped to minister to. This tribe had not been reached with the gospel, so their plan was to present it to them. Unfortunately, Jim and the other men were killed by tribesmen while trying to witness to the tribe.

Her husband's death left Elizabeth with a baby and no spouse to help. The very people they were trying to minister and witness to took someone very important from her. It is hard to imagine the pain she undoubtedly felt. But instead of anger and resentment, Elizabeth and her daughter eventually went live in the village of her husband's murderers. She refused to let her husband's tragedy keep her from continuing to find ways to minister and witness to that tribe. Years later, Elizabeth and the other widows who went live in the village saw the tribe come to faith in God.

Even in the midst of unspeakable tragedy, God was still at work. While it would be years before anyone would see what God was up to, God was in control and working through the deaths of Jim Elliott and other missionaries. Their deaths opened a door for the gospel and the salvation of many souls.

It would have been hard to imagine what God was going to accomplish in the lives of so many after the tragedy that befell the missionaries, but our lack of understanding does not limit God. He was still in control and worked it all out for the good of so many and His glory.

We may never know why God allows certain things to happen. We may never know all He accomplishes through the tragedies and difficulties we face, but isn't that the point of the promise God has given us through Habakkuk? Even though we can't see it or understand it, God is still working, and we can be confident He is working it all out in such a way that we wouldn't believe, even if we were told.

4
PLAN

If there was one way I was described over and over again as a child, it was that I was hardheaded. I guess I should be thankful I was called that instead of the many other things I could have (or maybe should have) been called, but it still is far from anything that could be considered a compliment. I have to admit, though, it was a pretty fair assessment. I am definitely stubborn and obstinate at times.

While being hardheaded may have headlined, that wasn't the only noteworthy personality trait I possessed. I was also very competitive and analytical. It didn't matter what I was doing; I was almost always competing. There are times when I look back and think, "Who was I competing against? Why was I even competing at all?" For the most part, I still don't have answers.

This competitive side put my analytical nature to good use, however. It didn't matter what I was doing; I was always analyzing things and looking for an edge. I loved figuring out how to get an advantage in any situation.

Growing up with this type of personality had its benefits. I was always decent at the sports I played. Also, I was able to maneuver my way through school and college without much issue. Nevertheless, there were drawbacks. Unfortunately, many people didn't have the sort of drive that pushed me to "win" at pretty much everything. Most people aren't viewing everything through a lens of competition and how to get the advantage, so there were some uncomfortable moments with others along the way.

I remember one example from my time in college that summarizes how I used to operate. My undergraduate degree was in business management, so I was required to take an advanced level management course before graduating. Near the end of my degree, I took this class, and to my surprise, the majority of your grade was determined by a group management project. For the project, your group was given a business in a virtual economy, and your goal was to have your business be as successful as possible. Pretty straightforward, right?

Now, for most students, this was just something to get done with your group in order to pass a class that was needed to graduate. For me, however, this became an opportunity to create the best business in the class. So, I got to work figuring out how everything worked and what the best strategy would be in order to establish the "winning" business.

You might have noticed I said it was a group project, and that's because it was. I was paired with a couple of other students randomly. Well, before this project kicked off, I made it abundantly clear to my groupmates that I was going to be the one in control of the business. I had a plan that would not only have us succeed, but I was positive my plan would ensure we would dominate the other groups. Before we officially started, though, one of my groupmates tried to make some changes to our business. I am sure this person was just curious how the dynamics of the program worked, or maybe this individual was interested in how the different metrics affected the business. This was an advanced management class, after all.

Whatever the reason, it wasn't going to fly with me. After a strong discussion where I reiterated my plan, we all agreed they would handle the other aspects of the project (e.g., writing the required paper) while I would take care of the business part.

The time eventually came for our businesses to launch in our virtual economy. I immediately went to work with the aim of cornering certain parts of the market. Very quickly, the business became a success and was dominating our part of the market. An A was certain.

At this point, most people would be content to take their grade on this important project and give their focus to other parts of the class. That wasn't me, though. I became bored with the success of our business, so I wondered what else this little company could do. Why did I have to only be successful in our part of the market? Why couldn't the business have the level of success in the entire market that I was enjoying in our small part of it?

With this newfound motivation, I was now determined to accomplish it. My mind was set, so I went to work figuring out a way to dominate the entire economy. The competitive juices were flowing, and I loved the challenge of analyzing everything in order to discover a way to reign supreme.

When all was said and done, I ended up doing just that. I quickly pivoted on a few things within the business and began to take over the rest of the market. I even made decisions that hurt our company in the short term in order to essentially put my other classmate's companies out of business completely. It was short-term pain for long-term supremacy.

The company became so successful that the professor ended up offering an extra credit assignment he never had to offer previously because I had pretty much bankrupted the rest of the class. The professor wasn't thrilled with the extra work, but he didn't feel like he had a choice due to the project essentially becoming a bloodbath.

So, why I am telling you this story? Is it to brag about this accomplishment? No, certainly not. As I look back at it, I definitely should have applied my Christian faith to the situation and not wrecked my classmates' projects. Is it to simply highlight what others could see as some major character issues? No. Thankfully, I have matured and changed over the years. I look back and shake my head as I am sure everyone else does as they read that story.

Really, the reason I bring up that story is that I am amazed by one part of it. Why in the world did my groupmates trust me and my plan? Honestly, to this day, I still don't understand how two other students could just let some guy they didn't know control such a large part of their academic future.

If I had bombed on the project, their grades would have greatly suffered. Despite it being different from how they would have run the project, they still trusted that it would all come together in a positive way (i.e., a high grade) despite not understanding what or why I was doing what I was doing.

All I can say is that my groupmates are better people than me. Yes, it all worked out, but there is no way I would have trusted some random stranger's plan. It was one of the last classes in our degrees, and a bad grade could have ruined everything. Still, they trusted me.

The Plan

When I think back on how I would have reacted if I was in my groupmate's shoes, I believe I get a glimpse into the mind of

Habakkuk as he hears God's response to his questions and complaint. To this point, we have seen two of the three parts of God's response. First, we saw the directive. Next, God gave Habakkuk an incredible promise. Now, God finally reveals His plan to deal with Habakkuk's complaint.

> [6] For behold, I am raising up the Chaldeans, that bitter and hasty nation, who march through the breadth of the earth, to seize dwellings not their own. [7] They are dreaded and fearsome; their justice and dignity go forth from themselves. [8] Their horses are swifter than leopards, more fierce than the evening wolves; their horsemen press proudly on. Their horsemen come from afar; they fly like an eagle swift to devour. [9] They all come for violence, all their faces forward. They gather captives like sand. [10] At kings they scoff, and at rulers they laugh. They laugh at every fortress, for they pile up earth and take it. [11] Then they sweep by like the wind and go on, guilty men, whose own might is their god!
>
> — Habakkuk 1:6–11

In this part of His response, God tells Habakkuk He has a plan to deal with the rampant injustice and wickedness that caused Habakkuk to question Him. God is raising up the Chaldeans (i.e., Babylonians), and they will be His instrument of judgment against His own people who have become so wicked and unjust.

What I find so interesting about these verses is the elongated description of the Babylonians God gives to Habakkuk. It's as if God is engrossed in how powerful and violent the instrument of His judgment is.

Taken in context, it seems God is bringing all this up about the Babylonians to allay Habakkuk's concerns. If Habakkuk was worried God was ignoring and not taking action against injustice and wickedness, God is telling Habakkuk that not only will He take action, but He will use a terrible and vile nation as His means of judgment against those things. He will use the power and brutality of this nation to strike a devastating blow.

With Habakkuk now learning God's plan, he seemed to be worried over nothing. God was and is working, so all Habakkuk needs to do is sit back and let God's plan play out.

This seems like a perfect place for the story to end, right? Habakkuk questioned God, God answered and demonstrated that Habakkuk's complaint was unfounded, and God even communicated some important lessons along the way. I'd say that is a great end to this story. Habakkuk can go home and forget all about his worries and complaints now. God's got this.

A New Complaint

Unfortunately, that isn't what happens in the story. As a matter of fact, it goes in the opposite direction. At this point, Habakkuk heard all God had to say regarding his questions and complaint. The God of the universe gave His prophet a response that incredibly provided a peek into His plans and how He was dealing with the ills Habakkuk brought to Him.

But Habakkuk isn't satisfied. He doesn't like God's response to his questions at all. As a matter of fact, Habakkuk now has a whole new complaint! And can you guess what this new complaint leads to? You guessed it—more questioning of God.

> ¹² Are you not from everlasting, O LORD my God, my Holy One? We shall not die. O LORD, you have ordained them as a judgment, and you, O Rock, have established them for reproof. ¹³ You who are of purer eyes than to see evil and cannot look at wrong, why do you idly look at traitors and remain silent when the wicked swallows up the man more righteous than he? ¹⁴ You make mankind like the fish of the sea, like crawling things that have no ruler. ¹⁵ He brings all of them up with a hook; he drags them out with his net; he gathers them in his dragnet; so he rejoices and is glad. ¹⁶ Therefore he sacrifices to his net and makes offerings to his dragnet; for by them he lives in luxury, and his food is rich. ¹⁷ Is he then to keep on emptying his net and mercilessly killing nations forever?
>
> — Habakkuk 1:12–17

God's plan to use the Babylonians in order to take care of the injustice and wickedness problem doesn't sit well with Habakkuk. Arguably, this revelation puts Habakkuk in a worse state than before. Once again, even though God affirmed to Habakkuk that He was working and even with Him pulling back the curtain to show how He was going to work, all it does is leave Habakkuk with a new complaint and more questions.

What Habakkuk's new complaint is centered around is

God's choice to use the Babylonians as His instrument of judgment. Habakkuk is dumbfounded by how God could possibly use a people like the Babylonians for anything, including punishing His own people.

In order to understand why Habakkuk is struggling with this revelation, we have to keep in mind what his original complaint and questions revolved around—injustice and wickedness. He approached God wanting an answer to the injustice and wickedness problem that was rampant all around him, but God's response was to use a nation that was known to be far more unjust and wicked as an instrument of judgment. This is what causes Habakkuk to renew his questioning of God. The plan God just revealed didn't make sense to Habakkuk.

As a matter of fact, not only does God's plan not make sense, but it appears to Habakkuk that God's plan will only be making the original issue worse. Think about everything from Habakkuk's point of view. If injustice and wickedness are the issues, how does allowing a nation that is more wicked than the one who will receive the judgment do anything to make things better? It only seems to make matters worse.

If Habakkuk was experiencing the wicked overtaking the righteous, isn't God's plan just more of the same but with different players? It involves the ones who were more wicked (the Babylonians) overtaking those who weren't nearly as bad (the people of Judah). How is that justice? It appears to only expand the problem to an even greater level!

Sure, God's people were in a pretty bad place, but the truth is they are nothing compared to the Babylonians. Even in their terrible state, the people of Judah could be considered righteous if someone directly compared them to the Babylonians. To Habakkuk, it seems as though God is not really resolving the issues he brought to Him originally. God gave him a response, but God's plan appeared to actually be exacerbating the issues further. The wicked will again triumph over the righteous, and it seems like more injustice will be the result.

Again, What Are You Doing, God?

So even though Habakkuk now has the assurance that God is working and will act decisively regarding his complaint, he is concerned the real problem isn't going to change. It appears to him that God's plan will simply result in more injustice and the wicked once again triumphing over the righteous. Simply put, Habakkuk can't understand or wrap his head around God's plan, so he continues to question God. Look at what Habakkuk says in this round of questioning:

> You who are of purer eyes than to see evil and
> cannot look at wrong, why do you idly look
> at traitors and remain silent when the
> wicked swallows up the man more righteous
> than he?
>
> — Habakkuk 1:13

In other words, if wickedness and injustice are affecting a sinful human like Habakkuk to where he would go so far as to question the one who is in control of all things, how can God, who is perfect, just, and infinitely pure, allow more injustice and wickedness to continue and even grow with His plan? How can this be reconciled? Habakkuk's understanding of a holy and powerful God doesn't appear to line up with what God said He will do. As a result, Habakkuk is so perturbed that he challenges God to answer his newest complaint.

> I will take my stand at my watchpost and station
> myself on the tower, and look out to see
> what he will say to me, and what I will
> answer concerning my complaint.
>
> — HABAKKUK 2:1

Habakkuk's posturing here is rather radical. He positions himself and says he will be waiting there for God to give him an answer. I imagine Habakkuk in his heart saying to God, "If you are the God that you declared to our fathers ... if you are the God who chose us as your people ... you need to answer for this. And I'll be right here waiting!"

While Habakkuk's actions indeed seem rather excessive and maybe even a little childish, they are also extremely bold and borderline stupid. I don't recommend following in Habakkuk's footsteps here. It is one thing to question God in moments of pain and disillusionment. It starts to edge closer and closer to crossing the line when we challenge God. Scripture is very clear we shouldn't be putting God to the test (Deut. 6:16, Lu. 4:12, 1 Cor. 10:9), so this shouldn't be taken as some prescribed way to get answers from God.

Instead, what I think this demonstrates is Habakkuk's humanity. Yes, he held a special position as a prophet of God, but he was still human. He was just as broken as all of us, and his response signals to us as the readers just how much he was bothered by God's plan. That God would use the Babylonians against His own people seems unconscionable. Habakkuk certainly wanted God to take action, but this? The whole scenario is so unimaginable to Habakkuk that he is now challenging God to answer.

If Habakkuk's first set of questions and complaint could be summarized by the question, "What are you doing, God?" the second complaint and questions can be summarized in the exact same way. If at first Habakkuk was trying to figure out what God was doing, now Habakkuk is trying to figure out why God is choosing to work in the way He has declared He will. Habakkuk is still left with the question, "What are you doing, God?"

Trust in God's Plan

One can read these verses and think that not much has happened since we see Habakkuk in a very similar place to where he started. Sure, God revealed His plan in response to Habakkuk's original complaint and questions, but all that did was lead to more questions. Again, it appears as though there wasn't a lot accomplished in these verses. In reality, though, God's plan and Habakkuk's subsequent response illuminate another important lesson.

Here is something I would say is true of most Christians. We believe if we just knew what God was up to then we would be OK. Yes, things may not be how we want them to be, but at least we would know what was going on through it all. The thought goes that if we knew, then we wouldn't complain and would be able to accept God's plan.

Unfortunately, God dismisses this notion with the promise He gave to Habakkuk. Remember, in the promise, God tells Habakkuk that he wouldn't believe what God was doing even if he was told. The same applies to us all. Even if we were told what God was doing in our day and in our situations, we would not believe it.

If you think this notion is nonsense or that you would somehow be different, all you have to do is look at Habakkuk's reaction to God's plan. It perfectly demonstrates the reality God made clear in His promise. Habakkuk's response becomes the archetype for everyone who questions God and thinks we would be OK if He simply told us what He was up to.

Look again at Habakkuk. God directly addressed his questions and complaint. Habakkuk was wondering why God was seemingly silent, but in His response, God tells Habakkuk that He was working. Habakkuk wonders why God is not doing anything about the injustice and wickedness that abound, but God tells Habakkuk that He has a plan to address it. And it will unfold through the Babylonians. It will be a harsh punishment on His people who have turned from Him.

But even though God answers Habakkuk and amazingly tells him how He will dole out His judgment, nothing in God's answer did anything to quell Habakkuk's concerns. Instead, knowing even a little of what God was planning made things worse for Habakkuk. Habakkuk went from questioning God to challenging Him for a response!

So as always, God's word is true, and it is demonstrated clearly for us in Habakkuk's story. Even knowing God's plan and how He was working to accomplish it did not ease Habakkuk's concerns. What we are left with is the bitter truth regarding the notion that all we need is to know what God is up to—it is completely unfounded.

This is where the next lesson emerges from the narrative. We have to trust in God's plan.

Now, you may be thinking, "Umm, alright. I already know it is important to trust in God's plan. This isn't some revolutionary thing." While that may be true, it isn't as easy as we often make it out to be. Once again, Habakkuk exemplifies this perfectly. Even if we apply the lessons we learned from the directive and promise—when we are at the place where we are questioning God, we need to change our perspective and realize our limitations—there is yet another place we can stumble.

Despite the incredible promise from verse five and even with God giving him the knowledge regarding how His plan would unfold, Habakkuk is still not satisfied. His complaint may have changed, but he is still questioning God. So, accepting the reality God is working and has a plan can be what steels many when they are faced with difficult situations, but even this truth and the promises that reaffirm it (e.g., Hab. 1:5 and Rom. 8:20) can still leave us wanting.

The reason our complaints and questions persist even in light of this reality is simple—we often question God regarding *how* He is working just as much as we question *if* He is working. This happens because we frequently don't like the way God seems to be working in what we are seeing and experiencing. We convince ourselves God should be working some other way.

When Christians think of God working in a situation, it is usually viewed through the lens of God turning things around in a way that betters our circumstances or results in some sort of blessing. That certainly can be what happens, but it also may not go the way we think it should. So yes, God will ultimately work out all things for our good and His glory, but we can't assume it will happen in the way we want.

If you are reading all of this and wondering what the difference is between what you read last chapter and what you're reading in this chapter, this is it. We can accept our limitations in understanding God and His plan while still not trusting in that plan. We all have plans for our lives, but the reality is that God's plan may be (and often is) different.

Now, in light of this reality, we can be like Habakkuk and get worked up and question God, or we can put aside our preferences, presuppositions, and thoughts of how things should go and trust in the one who holds the plan instead. We have to remember God's promises and trust in Him, knowing He is a good God (Ps. 119:68).

Meant It for Good

Easier said than done, right? Well, I believe there is encouragement throughout the pages of Scripture to help us with this struggle, and we will find it in the examples left for us. Through the stories of great men and women of faith, we can get a snapshot of how God often works.

There are scores of examples in the Bible of individuals going through extreme difficulty, and not one of them would have chosen for their stories to go the way they did. However, God used them powerfully despite circumstances that would have appeared impossible for anything good to come from them. These individuals may not have chosen their path for themselves, but God's plan for their lives turned out to better than they could have ever imagined.

One of the greatest examples of this is Joseph. Joseph was betrayed by his brothers, sold into slavery in a foreign nation, wrongfully accused, imprisoned for something he didn't do, and forgotten by a prisoner he helped. Any one of these things would have caused most of us to complain to and question God regarding His plan for our lives, but we have no record of Joseph doing that. Instead, Joseph continued to trust God, and he eventually ended up as one of the most powerful men in all of Egypt.

Later, Joseph is reunited with his brothers, and his brothers are obviously terrified by what he may do to them. Considering his position in this powerful empire and what they did to him years earlier, they think Joseph may retaliate. However, revenge was not on Joseph's mind. Instead, Joseph declares a powerful truth:

> As for you, you meant evil against me, but God meant it for good, to bring it about that many people should be kept alive, as they are today.
>
> — GENESIS 50:20

What an incredible statement. Joseph understood what was meant for evil, God ultimately turned into something that resulted not only in good for him but also for many others. I, like so many, love this verse. The truth behind it is powerful and encouraging. However, we can never forget the incredibly difficult journey it took to get Joseph to the place where he could declare those words.

I don't know a single Christian who doesn't want to stand victoriously over sin, evil, and our enemy. We want to declare them defeated and see God's power manifested in and through us. But almost no one wants to take the journey to get there. We all want the victory, but no one wants the trials. We all want the miracle, but no one wants to bear the cross. So often, we love the ending but not the journey.

That is because God's plans usually involve things we wouldn't sign off on. It may include paths we would never choose to take on our own. However, the beauty we see in the stories of Joseph and so many others recorded in Scripture is that God and His plans can be trusted.

He is doing a work in and around us that we wouldn't believe even if we knew, and it will all work out for the good of those who love Him and are called according to His purpose. So why do we still react like Habakkuk? Why do we still struggle with the way God is operating, even if we know how it will ultimately end?

The answer is that it is hard to come to grips with things not going how we planned. Also, it is difficult to walk through the tough seasons that inevitably come. During those times, it seems as though we are frequently left with unanswered questions. We struggle to understand what God's plan is and why it involves those aspects that don't fit with the plans we had for our lives. It often doesn't square away with our thoughts about how we hoped our lives would go. What is left to do in those moments? For many, we hurl our complaints and questions up to Him. Instead of trusting God's plan, we often trust our own understanding and plan for our lives.

In light of God's promise and His character, however, we should instead trust in God's plan and not our understanding or acceptance of it. Whether we understand it or not—whether we ever come to a place where we can accept the means and methods in which God is working—we have to fight our human nature that wants to complain and question God when things are going differently from how we think they should be. We have to remember the promise given to Habakkuk and trust God, knowing He is doing a work in our day and in our lives that we wouldn't believe.

In his response, Habakkuk proves God's promise to be true. God said he wouldn't believe if he was told, and when God told Habakkuk the plan, Habakkuk couldn't believe it. He couldn't believe God would choose to do things the way He planned to do them. Habakkuk couldn't understand it and certainly wasn't going to agree with it. The same is often true for us.

Again, we have to give up control regarding how we think our lives should go and trust in God. If we do this, we may not like what God is up to or ever agree with it, but we can find rest knowing the God of the universe is working in our situations and all around us. And through it all, if we remember the promise and learn to trust in God's plan, we can confidently stand before whatever we are facing and like Joseph declare:

> You meant evil against me, but God meant it for good.
>
> — Genesis 50:20

5

PATIENCE

Confession time. I am not patient. Well, I should say I am not as patient as I want to be. While I am a lot more than I was years ago, I'm still not there when it comes to this important aspect of the fruit of the spirit. I still constantly find myself getting impatient with even the simplest of things.

My kryptonite is traffic. I can be having the best day, but it will all be ruined by traffic, which I am convinced is one of the greatest signs of humanity's sinful fall. Having lived in many different cities, I understand there will be times when traffic is simply unavoidable. So, maybe I shouldn't put the blame for my impatience solely on traffic. Really, I think it is the different drivers you run into while in traffic that makes me have to repent for the things I think and want to say.

Even the smallest backup seems to cause people to immediately forget how to drive. All common sense and decency are thrown out and replaced with a *Mad Max*-type hellscape. Tailgating, people cutting other people off, passing on shoulders, and middle finger salutes are just a few of the things you will see as you navigate traffic. It's a wonder any of us survive.

What really gets me, however, are slow drivers that cause traffic. For instance, why does it always seem as if someone is going significantly slower in the left lane? Also, why are there so many drivers who change lanes in traffic at a much lower speed, causing others to have to slam on their brakes to avoid a crash? Every time I see an instance of things like this, I am saying something about the driver, but it is rarely a prayer. I'm joking (sort of), but you can still pray for me.

I don't know why these things bother me as much as they do because I am usually not pressed for time. In most instances, whatever inconvenience results from what I mentioned has little to no effect on what I am doing that day. However, I am still impatient and frustrated by the smallest instances of bad driving.

None of this even mentions trying to pick the correct lane to get in while in traffic. It is a guarantee that whatever lane I enter will immediately slow down or come to a stop while the other lane I just left will go faster. It's as if I am trapped in the opening scene from the movie *Office Space* over and over again. But I will catch myself at some point during my Sisyphus-like experience thinking, "What am I in a hurry for?"

Why in those moments and others am I so impatient? As I talk about this, I know I am not the only one who struggles with patience. It seems to be a common problem. Even if it happens only occasionally, I think most of us struggle with being impatient. Patience may be a virtue, but it is one many of us are lacking.

This lack of patience can have repercussions for our lives outside of frustration from traffic, though. It can also have quite an effect on our spiritual lives. As we will see, God eventually brings Habakkuk's focus to this important reality.

. . .

A Vision

We were left with Habakkuk challenging God to respond to his newest questions and complaint. After this kind of challenge, anyone reading would be anxious to see how God responds. Habakkuk was blessed to have God respond directly to his original questions and complaint, but with this new set of questions and the challenge he issued to God, one could expect Him to not be as generous.

When I first read how Habakkuk came back at God after He graciously responded the first time, I assumed God would punish Habakkuk. There is no record that Habakkuk sinned in doing what he did, but it is definitely not the way to respond to God, especially after He responded directly to you. My guess was God would have answered by striking the prophet with some sort of illness or other physical ailments (personally, I think hurling lighting is severely underused by God). But God doesn't respond that way at all.

Instead, God's response demonstrates the reality He is about to reveal to Habakkuk. God responds with patience toward His questioning prophet. Instead of smiting or scolding him, God is gracious to Habakkuk and gives him another answer.

However, this answer is much different than His first response, and it goes far beyond demonstrating patience. Instead of simply responding to his questions and complaint, God will give Habakkuk a vision. In this vision, God will reveal an incredible truth that is of extreme importance for Habakkuk. Before getting to any of that, though, it is important to look closely at what God says leading up to this truth and the reality it declares.

> ² And the LORD answered me: "Write the vision; make it plain on tablets, so he may run who reads it. ³ For still the vision awaits its appointed time; it hastens to the end—it will not lie. If it seems slow, wait for it; it will surely come; it will not delay.
>
> — HABAKKUK 2:2–3

Verse three is a bridge that begins to bring all the different threads together. It is a lesson that connects God's first response with the vision He is about to reveal.

Remember, God told Habakkuk in His original response He would use the Babylonians as an instrument of judgment against His own people. This obviously didn't sit well with Habakkuk. Habakkuk couldn't wrap his head around how doing that would solve the injustice and wickedness problem. All it seemed to do was exacerbate it with more injustice and wickedness because the Babylonians were far worse than God's own people. Yet God was still planning to hand them over to the Babylonians.

In Habakkuk's mind, this not only isn't an acceptable solution, but it continues the very problem that led him there in the first place. And this doesn't even mention how incongruent what God revealed seemed to be with the promise He gave to His people previously:

> For you are a people holy to the LORD your God, and the LORD has chosen you to be a people for his treasured possession, out of all the peoples who are on the face of the earth.

— Deuteronomy 14:2

How can God allow His "treasured possession" to be invaded by a people who serve other gods and are worse than they are? What about the other promises concerning God's plan for His people? How can all of that happen if His people are destroyed? Habakkuk couldn't see or understand how everything would work out.

God in His infinite wisdom knew the apparent incongruity at times between what He previously said and what would be currently playing out in the world and people's lives wouldn't just be an issue for Habakkuk. This is what makes the start to God's newest response extremely noteworthy.

God is building on what He previously said to Habakkuk by telling him that He has appointed a time for everything (2:3). In His earlier response, God revealed He had a plan for all that happens, and at the beginning of this response, God is telling Habakkuk those plans and everything else that has and will happen have their appointed times. All things are moving according to God's overall plan toward their determined outcomes in exactly the moment He appoints for them.

This would clearly include what God already revealed through His words and promises, such as the promise above from Deuteronomy and the promise Habakkuk was just given. Habakkuk needs to remember that God is in control of all things, including what seems terrible or evil. Because of this, Habakkuk can be sure everything will go exactly how God has planned it in exactly the timing He has determined.

The end of all things will come and play out perfectly according to what God wills. In addressing Habakkuk, God even says he can take this reality to the bank—whatever revelation or promise God gives will not turn out to be a lie but will absolutely be true.

This leads into the second part of verse three, which is the core tenet of what God is revealing to Habakkuk here. It also gives us another important lesson we can learn and apply to our lives.

Be Patient

> If it seems slow, wait for it; it will surely come; it will not delay.
>
> — HABAKKUK 2:3

As I said from the start, impatience is a prominent issue for most people, but it is especially prevalent when we are talking about God interacting with humans. When God has promised or said He will do something, we can easily get impatient, wanting to know when it will happen or why it hasn't happened yet. Really, we want things to happen immediately or on our own timetable. The problem is, though, that God operates on a completely different one. God has already determined what the end of all things and every situation will be, and He will have it unfold when He decides, not when we want it to.

God is not beholden to us to have things go the way we want or for them to happen when we want them to, even though that would certainly be our preference. God is God, and we are not. He doesn't owe us anything, including an explanation for His actions and a convenient unveiling of them that works best for us and our schedules.

God gives this reminder to Habakkuk and has him memorialize it as an important preface to what is coming. Just because something hasn't happened yet or it seems to be taking forever to unfold, never think that means it won't. God's word will always be true. His promises are sure. Any delay or apparent lack of resolution should not cause us to lose heart or abandon our trust in what God has said.

So, the lesson for us is the same as it was for Habakkuk and his original audience—whatever we are waiting for that God has promised or declared will surely come. Its end is certain. Sure, it may be taking longer than we want, but we should never think it won't happen or that it is even delayed. God's will for all things is unfolding exactly and purposefully according to His plan.

The Bible gives us a tremendous example and explanation of this reality in the book of 2 Peter. In it, Peter is fighting back against "scoffers" who are questioning the second coming and final judgment. They are basically asking, "If God promised all this, where is He?" Look at how Peter responds:

> [8] But do not overlook this one fact, beloved, that with the Lord one day is as a thousand years and a thousand years as one day. [9] The Lord is not slow to fulfill his promise as some count slowness but is patient toward you, not wishing that any should perish, but that all should reach repentance.
>
> — 2 Peter 3:8–9

Peter gets to the heart of the issue right away—how we experience time is completely different from how God does. Time itself is part of His creation, so there is no comparison between how God perceives time compared to us. Peter expounds on this by pointing out that long periods of time such as thousands of years are like an instant to God and vice versa.

What is interesting is that Peter is quoting Psalm 90 when he makes this point. By doing this, Peter is reminding the people of what they already know. He isn't revealing something they weren't aware of; they would have known this because the idea was previously memorialized in that psalm.

In order to illustrate why this is important to remember and not forget, Peter turns his attention to the scoffers and their issues with the second coming and judgment. He makes the point that, sure, it may seem slow or delayed, but what is really happening is it's all simply part of God's greater plan to allow more people to repent and come to Him. It all has a purpose, even what seems like an apparent delay. In light of this, there isn't a single follower of God who would say a delay that allows more people to come to Him is a bad thing.

Once again, they knew this about God. It was in a psalm they would have heard since childhood, but as is often the case, we can forget these simple truths about God, especially when what we want doesn't line up with God's plan. We can become so impatient as a result. But by being impatient, we can lose sight of how God's plan could be unfolding in a different but positive way. In the example Peter used, this "delay" was actually planned in order for more people to receive salvation.

While we can understand and see the need for patience in an example where patience can lead to other's eternal souls being saved, we often struggle mightily with patience when it comes to God moving in other areas of our lives. This rings especially true when we find ourselves in a place where we are questioning Him.

It can be disheartening to know God, recognize His character and power, but not see Him working in the world or the situations we are facing. It challenges and, at times, frustrates us. However, God doesn't have to meet our deadlines or expectations. He is still God, and we are not. That means His timing for things will often not be our timing.

Instead, God has a perfect plan that is unfolding just as He prepared from the beginning of time itself. Don't think anything God has said or promised is actually delayed or not coming. It will happen exactly when He planned it to.

All of this is why God tells Habakkuk to memorialize these things. It is something we all need to be reminded of constantly as we follow God.

If Habakkuk had been patient from the beginning, he probably wouldn't have questioned God. He didn't understand why God wasn't intervening to stop the injustice and wickedness all around him, but he learned God had a plan for it. Sure, it was unfolding slower and in a different way than he wanted, but God had a plan that would surely come to pass.

Now, God is about to reveal something crucial, and He doesn't want Habakkuk to make the same mistake. When God gives him the upcoming vision, it will be easy for Habakkuk to slip into the same trap of impatience as he did before, so God is prefacing everything that will be revealed with this important lesson—be patient.

As this chapter closes, I know it is rather short and the lesson is pretty simple, but don't skip over it or move quickly past it. Yes, next chapter is where this biblical book starts to go deeper and get meatier, but don't be *impatient* and just rush on to that chapter. While the lesson can seem rather rudimentary, there is great wisdom hidden in its simplicity. We shouldn't overlook it. If we do, we can find ourselves once again where Habakkuk found himself.

We can get worked up and begin to question God over something He is already taking care of. His plan for your life or circumstances could already be unfolding as you read this, but we can fall into the terrible habit of constantly complaining because we are simply being impatient regarding the timing of how God is letting it all unfold.

Sure, patience isn't easy, especially if you are in the middle of difficult times or a challenging situation. You can know God has a plan and a purpose for your life, but you can also find yourself wondering why that thing you are praying for or believing will happen is taking so long.

Here is our reminder, though. Again, God is still God, and we are not. You may not like what you are walking through or the timing of it all, but let these verses remind you of this critical reality. God not only has a plan for you, but He is working it out in His perfect timing. Any sort of waiting we have to do or apparent silence by God isn't because God is blowing you off or delaying. Instead, it is actually all part of His plan.

We can rail against it, be mad, and drive ourselves crazy trying to figure it all out, or we can embrace this reality. If we do embrace it, we can find rest and even peace instead of worry. We can find solace knowing that even the silence is part of God's perfect plan. God is working it all together for our good and His glory.

Yes, being patient isn't easy. I am still pointlessly changing lanes, trying to save maybe a minute or two. However, this lesson is worth remembering and applying to our lives. I love what Isaiah 40:31 says:

> But they who wait for the LORD shall renew their strength; they shall mount up with wings like eagles; they shall run and not be weary; they shall walk and not faint.
>
> — Isaiah 40:31

Patience is never fun, but waiting for God can actually give you the strength and endurance to walk through any and every dark time. In your life, when you are facing whatever is causing you to question God, remember this lesson. Trust in God's plan and be patient. Remember what God said to His prophet:

> It hastens to the end—it will not lie. If it seems slow, wait for it; it will surely come; it will not delay.
>
> — Habakkuk 2:3

6
PRIDE

I love to travel. Over the years, visiting new places has become a major hobby of mine. When this book is published, I will have visited almost every continent and all the states here in America. While there isn't really an overarching plan to how I choose where I will go and what I will do next, there is one specific thing I like to do at the end of every major trip—end it on a beach.

I love the beach, and it is hard for me to imagine how some people don't. I love relaxing with my toes in the sand as I hear the waves crash onto the shore and feel the breeze blow by. I'm convinced it is a taste of heaven.

To be clear, though, as I am relaxing on the beach at the end of my trip, I loved and had a blast visiting all the places that came before this last stop. I don't want anyone to think the beach somehow diminished all those experiences for me. Rather, making a final stop to relax on a beach has become a tradition that I feel perfectly punctuates my adventures.

It doesn't matter if it was Bondi Beach in Australia, a beach in the United Arab Emirates, or something closer to home like Cabo San Lucas, my last stop on a beach has turned into the heart of every trip. No matter where in the world I wandered, all roads eventually led back to the beach.

In a way, this is where we have arrived in the book of Habakkuk. Everything before this has been extremely important and contained some very valuable lessons. If we took and applied those lessons to our lives, I think most of us would be happy and rather satisfied with what we learned from this book of the Bible.

Now, however, we have arrived at a critical juncture in the book. All roads in our journey have led us to this vital point. We can love every stop we've taken on this journey so far, but if we miss what is coming, we are missing out on so much. Everything to this point has set up what is about to happen, so we better pay attention to it and what it means. If we don't, we are actually missing the very heart of Habakkuk's book.

The Heart

Habakkuk's questions and complaints have boiled over into him challenging God and waiting for God to answer. As we saw, God started His newest response by telling Habakkuk that he needed to be patient—all things are moving toward their appointed end. Even if something seems slow, its result will come. God doesn't lie, so you can bank on the outcome.

Why would this be the start of God's response, though? It seems like an odd start to any answer until you see and understand what God says next:

> Behold, his soul is puffed up; it is not upright
>   within him, but the righteous shall live by
>   his faith.

— Habakkuk 2:4

This is the central point of the entire book. In this verse, God gives Habakkuk a timeless truth, "The righteous shall live by faith." This truth is so important that it has echoed throughout the ages. Even if you are just casually reading this book of the Bible, this truth would undoubtedly draw your focus.

But this truth is only part of verse four. It is obviously the most well-known part, but it only makes up half of what God is communicating. Without understanding the entire verse, it is easy to miss the context of why God is giving this truth and what it means with regard to answering Habakkuk's newest complaint and questions.

When looking at the entire verse, you begin to see something rather interesting—a contrast. God puts forward two different people. First, God talks about someone whose "soul is puffed up; it is not upright within him." In other words, God is talking about a prideful person. After, God talks about the person who is righteous. Simply put, what God is doing here is pointing out that there are essentially two types of people when it comes to dealing with difficulties and disappointments—the proud and the righteous.

This contrast is unbelievably important. To misunderstand or not grasp what God is communicating through it would be to miss the totality of the truth God reveals in this book of the Bible. Really, with this verse, everything begins to fall into place. Through this contrast, God begins to bring everything into alignment as he unfolds a beautiful response to all of Habakkuk's questions and complaints.

Before piecing it all together, however, I want to take the time to really dive into this contrast God is making when He puts forward these two different people. I believe it is worth focusing on why God gives Habakkuk this contrast and what it means for us. In this chapter, we are going to explore what God was communicating when He highlights the proud person.

Pride

God spends most of His second response to Habakkuk focusing on the proud person. But what does this person look like and, maybe at a more basic level, what is pride? If God contrasts righteousness with it, it must be noteworthy. Look at how God starts His explanation of the proud person in verse five:

> Moreover, wine is a traitor, an arrogant man who is never at rest. His greed is as wide as Sheol; like death he has never enough. He gathers for himself all nations and collects as his own all peoples.
>
> — HABAKKUK 2:5

In explaining what the proud person looks like, God begins to talk about a "man" who acts a certain way and does specific things such as "gather for himself all nations." A question naturally follows: Who is this "man" God is referencing?

It turns out, God is talking about the Babylonians. While it isn't immediately clear, when one looks at the entire chapter, this is certainly who God is referencing. What God is doing here is rather interesting as He associates the Babylonians and the proud person. God is putting the Babylonians forward as an example of pride.

God does this for an important reason. Connecting the Babylonians to the proud person allows God to easily illuminate different traits that define a proud person. Simply discussing pride and a proud person as general ideas would be rather difficult. Most of us understand these terms in one way or another, but they are also a little abstract. Talking about them generally can lead to misunderstandings regarding what God is communicating. This is why He offers us the Babylonians as a tangible example of what pride and a proud person look like and what results from them.

So, look at what God says about pride and the proud person through His use of the Babylonians as the embodiment of these ideas. Back to verse five, God talks about the Babylonians as an arrogant man who never rests. Why is this the case? Because he never has enough. His appetite is like death in that it is never satisfied. Death never reaches a limit on how many people it will claim, and the proud person similarly will never have enough. There always has to be more. That is why the Babylonians continue to invade and conqueror nation after nation. One would think they would eventually be satisfied, but they are never content with their conquests. The Babylonians continue their fruitless and never-ending desire to overthrow nations.

In order to grasp why this insatiable appetite results from pride, you have to understand something basic about all humans. While we were created to glorify God, He also created us to be creatures who respond to Him in worship. We were made to respond in reverence and adoration when we experience God and the attributes of who He is, such as His power, magnificence, revelation, and the awe-inspiring nature of how He created everything.

Well, when pride starts to infect our lives as it did with the Babylonians, we run into a problem. Pride causes us to look for something to worship outside of God. But everything other than God that we worship always turns out to be lacking. We may fool ourselves into thinking something else will be the thing that fulfills us and our base need to worship, but whatever we substitute for God never does. As a result, our worship of anything other than God ends up being fleeting.

After our worship of something other than God turns out to be insufficient, we inevitably end up moving on to the next thing to worship. And when that thing comes up lacking, we move on to the next. This cycle continues on and on and on. Since worship is a part of the very fabric of who we are, we can never stop in our pursuit of trying to find something worthy of our worship. We are never truly fulfilled until we do.

We search and search for the thing, experience, person, feeling, or whatever else we think will give us satisfaction or ultimate fulfillment, but we eventually find out there is nothing that can give us what we were made to have when we experience and worship God. We constantly labor to locate anything we can give our worship to and discover fulfillment as a result, but we never find it in our own prideful pursuits.

So, God's discussion of the proud person starts with this disastrous result of pride—the proud person will never obtain rest in his pursuit to find something that will provide ultimate satisfaction. It will never happen because we were made to worship God instead of our worship going to other things.

God's discussion of the proud person doesn't stop here, however. With the rest of His response, God will continue to use the Babylonians as an example of a proud person and what results from their pride. Really, verse five sets up everything else that follows. If verse five shows us that the proud person will be fruitless in his pursuit to find something that will satisfy his God-given desire to worship, the verses that follow demonstrate some of the things we all pursue thinking they will provide ultimate satisfaction.

It's as if God knows we may not believe Him as He discusses pride and the dangers of it. For many, if not most of us, simply pointing out the problem and danger the proud person faces wouldn't be enough, so God begins to direct our attention to some of the most common things we as humans pursue thinking they will satisfy us.

The Woes

God is going to accomplish this by presenting these various pursuits as a series of woes against the Babylonians. He highlights the specific pursuits the Babylonians are guilty of and what the result is. In doing this, anyone who reads Habakkuk's book will see what results from pride and these pursuits.

The first and second woe deal with money, resources, and greed.

> Woe to him who heaps up what is not his own—
> for how long?— and loads himself with
> pledges!
>
> — Habakkuk 2:6

> Woe to him who gets evil gain for his house, to
> set his nest on high, to be safe from the
> reach of harm!
>
> — Habakkuk 2:9

God points out a very common way we as humans try to find fulfillment and satisfaction in this life—through money and resources. The pursuit of money or resources (whatever that may be) is a driver for many people. The prevailing sentiment is that if we just get a certain amount of money or possessions, then we will be satisfied and fulfilled.

That simply isn't the case, though. There is no amount of money, resources, or possessions that will ever fully satisfy us. Though many direct their worship and energy to these things, they are still ultimately left wanting. What results instead of fulfillment and satisfaction is greed, and the Babylonians provide a great example of this on two different levels.

First, verse six shows us the danger individually, while verse nine highlights it corporately. In both instances, the great wealth and prosperity of Babylon aren't enough. If our money and resources were able to provide some sort of ultimate satisfaction or fulfillment, surely a place like Babylon would have reached it. Instead, the Babylonians continue to invade other nations and carry off the spoils of their conquests. They never reach a point where they have enough.

In these verses, God is showing that greed has infected the Babylonians. They continue to take what is not theirs. Whether it was through their conquests or from other theft, the people load themselves up. Their gains are unjust and described as evil, and it seems to never stop.

Unfortunately, there is another side effect of greed besides never providing satisfaction or fulfillment. As our greed causes us to gain more money and more resources, we begin to think these things will provide us a certain level of protection. In verse nine, though, God mocks the Babylonians because they think they are protected and safe from harm due to what they possess.

God goes on to show the result of this prideful pursuit. Not only is there no satisfaction, but there is also no safety. The things the Babylonians have done to others will eventually happen to them. They will eventually be plundered (vv. 7–8) and destroyed in disgrace (vv. 10–11). They will be brought low as they have done to others.

Though having money, resources, and possessions may seem like a great way to satisfy us and provide us with fulfillment, it doesn't. Like the Babylonians, when our pride results in greed, we will eventually reap what we sow. And even though our money and resources can insulate or shield us from many bad things, their protection won't last. Eventually, our money can only do so much, and we will face the same fate as the Babylonians.

The third woe deals with power.

> Woe to him who builds a town with blood and
> founds a city on iniquity!
>
> — HABAKKUK 2:12

The Babylonians flaunt their power and might. Their nation and great cities are built on violence and wickedness. If, as the saying goes, "might makes right," then no one could accuse the Babylonians of being wrong.

Our pride can lead us to think what we need is more power or more prestige. Maybe it is positional, relational, vocational, or something else, but we convince ourselves that achieving a certain level of prestige or a higher level of influence will satisfy us. The result of this pursuit is similar to the last. No amount of power or influence will matter in the end because whatever we achieve is nothing in comparison to God. The Babylonians again become a perfect example of this. They flaunt their power and might, but look at what God says about it:

> For the earth will be filled with the knowledge
> of the glory of the LORD as the waters
> cover the sea.
>
> — Habakkuk 2:14

Ultimately, when all is said and done, will the earth remember the great might of the Babylonians? No. In the end, God's glory and power will be what fills the earth. The Babylonians will face the mighty power of God just like all other nations who didn't follow Him.

This means that pursuing power, prestige, or influence is a fruitless endeavor because it lacks lasting value. Even the most powerful people and nations will fade because they are nothing compared to the eternal glory and power of our God.

What then becomes the point of trying to go for more of those things when we can serve the one who has ultimate power? Why, if we are committed to following God, would we try to get more of it when we have the example of the King of kings, Jesus, laying aside His power for us (Phil. 2:6–9)? We will never find fulfillment grasping for more power and prestige.

The fourth woe deals with pleasure and debauchery.

> Woe to him who makes his neighbors drink—
> you pour out your wrath and make them
> drunk, in order to gaze at their nakedness!
>
> — Habakkuk 2:15

If all else fails, do what makes you happy, right? The pursuit of happiness in pleasure seems as old as time itself, but it also cannot satisfy us or provide fulfillment. The Babylonians enjoyed debauchery and pressed others into joining them in their indulgences. They participated in things such as drunkenness, sex, and other pleasures and led those around them in pursuit of the same things.

The result of the Babylonian's pursuit of pleasure will be anything but pleasing. Instead of the glory and joy they received from all the debauchery they indulged in and forced on others, they will receive shame. They may have enjoyed what was in their cups while they were drinking it, but they will not enjoy what is in God's cup when He pours out His wrath on them (v. 16).

For us, though our world is fixated on promoting the pursuit of every pleasure and desire one imagines, we will never find satisfaction or fulfillment in it. Sure, for a time it can seem as though we couldn't be more satisfied as we obtain what we desire, but that momentary pleasure will fade. What we will be left with is what so many, including the Babylonians generations ago, were left with—shame.

To this point, all four woes demonstrate what God revealed about the proud person originally—the proud person will never obtain satisfaction or fulfillment through finding something of his own choosing to worship. Though he thinks he can, the proud person's pursuit will fail to find the thing that will satisfy his God-given desire to worship.

Idolatry

The final woe God gives is different than all the others. With this woe, God gets to the heart of the pride issue. Everything else to this point described the proud person, but now God is going to show what pride really is and why it is so destructive.

> [18] What profit is an idol when its maker has shaped it, a metal image, a teacher of lies? For its maker trusts in his own creation when he makes speechless idols! [19] Woe to him who says to a wooden thing, Awake; to a silent stone, Arise! Can this teach? Behold, it is overlaid with gold and silver, and there is no breath at all in it.
>
> — Habakkuk 2:18–19

God here lays it out bare. He gets right to the real issue with pride, which is idolatry. In these verses, God is pointing out the foolishness of creating idols. In our search for something to worship, if we can't find anything that will satisfy our God-given desire, we will ultimately create something to give our worship to. But what is it we are worshipping when we create these idols? Think of a physical idol that many would have had in that day. It would have been some material made into an image (e.g., an animal, person, some other creature), and the person who owned the idol would worship that image.

To get that idol, however, someone would obviously have to make it. The book of Isaiah gives a great breakdown of the absurdity of this reality and why it is important:

> [13] The carpenter stretches a line; he marks it out with a pencil. He shapes it with planes and marks it with a compass. He shapes it into the figure of a man, with the beauty of a man, to dwell in a house. [14] He cuts down cedars, or he chooses a cypress tree or an oak and lets it grow strong among the trees of the forest. He plants a cedar and the rain

nourishes it. ¹⁵ Then it becomes fuel for a
man. He takes a part of it and warms
himself; he kindles a fire and bakes bread.
Also, he makes a god and worships it; he
makes it an idol and falls down before it. ¹⁶
Half of it he burns in the fire. Over the half
he eats meat; he roasts it and is satisfied.
Also, he warms himself and says, "Aha, I am
warm, I have seen the fire!" ¹⁷ And the rest
of it he makes into a god, his idol, and falls
down to it and worships it. He prays to it
and says, "Deliver me, for you are my god!"

— Isaiah 44:13–17

Isaiah highlights the absurdity of humans creating something to worship by using the example of a carpenter. With the same wood, the carpenter would warm himself and also create something to worship. He elevates part of the wood by creating an image he will give his worship to, but with the other part, he burns it to cook his meal. How can half of the wood be used to cook a meal while the other half be worthy of worship? It truly is ludicrous!

While we may laugh at the ridiculousness of it, we all do the same thing even today. We take something that, most of the time, isn't a bad thing (it is often actually good!), and we elevate it to a place where we have convinced ourselves it is worthy of our worship. Of course, most people aren't making physical idols anymore, but we are all still constantly creating idols from things around us and giving them our worship. Paul hits on this reality in his letter to the church in Colossae:

Put to death therefore what is earthly in you:

> sexual immorality, impurity, passion, evil desire, and covetousness, which is idolatry.
>
> — COLOSSIANS 3:5

Paul links covetousness (an excessive desire for something) with idolatry. What Paul does here is similar to what God gives to Habakkuk in His woes directed at the Babylonians. Anything we want—that we excessively desire—over and above what God has intended for us (e.g., money, sex, power, renown, possessions, happiness, comfort, spouse, family, job, etc.), even if it is a good thing, actually becomes an idol for us. We convince ourselves that thing will give us satisfaction and fulfillment, so we end up giving it our worship.

Now that we understand a bit more regarding idolatry and our worship, look at how it all begins to connect with pride. Go back to what God said to Habakkuk in verse eighteen: What profit are idols since someone has to create them? It is ultimately nothing but a created thing—an idol we often create by elevating something in our lives over and above what God intended for us—yet we still convince ourselves it is worthy of worship. Even though we are the ones elevating it, we still fool ourselves into thinking it will somehow provide ultimate satisfaction and fulfillment!

This is what we do when we make idols. We choose to create these idols—whether they are made of wood or come from our desires—and then worship them as though they deserve it. It is rather silly when you think about it, but we continue to do it over and over again. Even though we know so many things we chase after won't fulfill us, we continue our pursuit of them, make them idols by elevating their place in our lives, and worship them.

. . .

Self-Worship / Elevating Ourselves

Really, if you dive a little deeper below the surface, when we create these idols and then worship them—when we constantly go through this cycle—what is happening is actually just self-worship. Let me explain what I mean by that.

When we create an idol and worship it, what we're actually doing is worshipping ourselves. The reason this is the case is that whatever your idol may be is simply an extension of yourself. Think about it. It doesn't matter what idol we are worshipping; we created that idol, and we did it by elevating something above God in our lives. These idols are extensions of our hopes, desires, wants, or whatever else. So, when we worship these things, we are simply worshipping ourselves and what we want through whatever it is we have chosen to elevate above God. Instead of giving our worship to God, who rightfully deserves it, we instead choose to worship something made in our own image and from our own desires.

Sure, we were made to respond to God in worship, but through our pride, we have determined something else deserves our worship more than Him. We convince ourselves that if we just had this or could get more of that, we would find the satisfaction and fulfillment we were made to have when we rightfully give God our worship. In a very real way, when we chose something to elevate and worship, we are determining what is best for our own lives.

Again, we make this choice over and above what God has determined we should worship (which is Him), so in essence, we are usurping God's authority as the Creator and making ourselves like God. When we create these idols, we have determined right and wrong for ourselves by elevating something in our lives we have decided will receive our worship instead of God.

If some of that language sounds familiar, it probably should. It directly echoes the first temptation and sin. In the garden, God instructed Adam and Eve to not eat the fruit of the tree of the knowledge of good and evil. That was their only restriction. Then the serpent appeared to tempt them, and look at how he does it:

> [1] Now the serpent was more crafty than any other beast of the field that the LORD God had made. He said to the woman, "Did God actually say, 'You shall not eat of any tree in the garden'?" [2] And the woman said to the serpent, "We may eat of the fruit of the trees in the garden, [3] but God said, 'You shall not eat of the fruit of the tree that is in the midst of the garden, neither shall you touch it, lest you die.'" [4] But the serpent said to the woman, "You will not surely die. [5] For God knows that when you eat of it your eyes will be opened, and you will be like God, knowing good and evil."
>
> — Genesis 3:1–5

Verse five is the key to the temptation. The serpent tells them, if they take and eat the fruit, they will be like God. They don't have to be satisfied with what God has for them and His plan for their lives (i.e., not eating the fruit). They can elevate themselves beyond what God has determined for their lives and the boundaries He has in place for them. Also, they can know good and evil. In other words, instead of simply relying on God and abiding by His moral restrictions, they can determine what is right and wrong for themselves since they will also know good and evil.

This is why pride and the idolatry that stems from it are so devastating. At its heart, pride is the unwarranted elevating of oneself. I love the way Augustine talked about pride in His work *The City of God*:

> *And what is the origin of our evil will but pride? For "pride is the beginning of sin." And what is pride but the craving for undue exaltation? And this is undue exaltation, when the soul abandons Him to whom it ought to cleave as its end, and becomes a kind of end to itself.*
>
> (Quoted in Philip Schaff, *Nicene and Post-Nicene Fathers* [New York: Cosimo Classics, 2007], 273)

What Augustine discusses is critically important to understand. Pride isn't just something bad or simply a sin. It is the beginning of sin. As we saw, when Adam and Eve faced the original temptation, they were tempted to elevate themselves to the level of God. If they ate the fruit, they could be like God; they could determine good and evil.

This is at the heart of sinful pride—elevating ourselves to the level of God. It was the beginning of sin, and it has infected all humans. Every single one of us has a sinful nature, and within that sinful nature, the first temptation comes up over and over again in our lives and everything we do. Humans have always wanted to rise above our limitations and be like God. We want to determine what is right and wrong for ourselves. We want the final say on what our lives ultimately look like. We want to be the ones who control our destiny.

In other words, we want to be the god of our lives. And part of that is making the determination for ourselves what will receive our worship. Our pride won't have us be limited to our original design, which is to worship God and God alone as a response to Him. Even though it is in the very fabric of how we were created, we still want to make the choice for ourselves what receives our worship.

As the Creator of all things, God is the one who rightfully determines what we should worship, but in our pride, we throw off the bounds of how we're created. We usurp the true Creator's design by elevating ourselves to the level of creator in our own lives. We do this by choosing to create (or elevate) something of our choosing that we decide will be the object of our worship instead of God. All of this becomes just a roundabout way to worship ourselves as the god of our lives.

Maybe you read this and don't think any of it is really that bad, but the real problem lies in the fact that we make terrible gods. The reason we make terrible gods isn't just because we will inevitably make decisions that are not best for us and our future (even though we will definitely make those decisions). The real reason we make terrible gods goes back again to how we were created—we were made to glorify and give our worship to God as a response to Him. However, the sinful pride we all have within us is constantly looking to something else besides God to worship, leaving us dissatisfied and unfulfilled.

To bring it up once again, the vicious cycle of us making an idol, worshipping it, realizing it will never fully satisfy, and then starting all over again by creating a new idol continues on and on. Honestly, if you want to understand why so many are hopeless, look no further than this terrible cycle. No matter how many times you go through it, you will always find yourself lacking and having to locate something new to worship. You will always have to elevate something else and, by doing that, make a new idol. There is never any true satisfaction or fulfillment.

Everything I discussed helps us understand what God

means when He talks about the proud person. The pride at the heart of this person removes God from His rightful place and elevates himself as god over his life and what he will worship, which simply ends up being himself through various idols.

The Result of Pride / An Answer to Habakkuk

To this point, we have covered a lot of ground regarding what God means when He is talking about pride and the proud person. However, there is another side to this coin that is extremely important for us to understand.

God didn't simply choose the Babylonians because they provide an excellent representation of what pride and a proud person really are. There was another reason God chose to put forward the Babylonians as an example, and that reason deals specifically with Habakkuk's latest complaint and questions.

Through His use of the Babylonians as an example of the proud person, God is actually answering Habakkuk's newest complaint. Habakkuk questioned how God could use a nation as evil and wicked as the Babylonians against His own people, but God's discussion of the proud person shows Habakkuk that the Babylonians would face their own judgment. God's people are facing judgment at the hands of the Babylonians for their injustice and wickedness, while the Babylonians' judgment, in part, will result from their pride.

Though we have already seen some bad outcomes that result from pride, all of these outcomes can be boiled down to one general result for pride—destruction. Proverbs gives us this clear outcome of pride when it communicates that "pride goes before destruction" (Prov. 16:18). Destruction is the ultimate end for the proud, and Babylonians will not be an exception.

Their pride and sin highlighted by God in His description of the proud person will result in their eventual downfall and destruction.

Again, this is important for us to understand. In His response, God is not only giving us a look into who the proud person is and what results from his pride, but He is also addressing Habakkuk's concerns regarding His use of the Babylonians as an instrument of His judgment. He is showing that, as the embodiment of the proud person, the Babylonians will face disaster just as all proud people will. Their end is sure, and it is destruction.

This is also why God introduces the contrast we have been looking at in verse four with the reminder regarding patience. Habakkuk now knows the Babylonians' end is sure; they will face judgment and destruction. So, Habakkuk needs to remember what God said in verse three: "If [the Babylonian's judgment and destruction] seems slow, wait for it; it will surely come; it will not delay" (2:3).

So once again, Habakkuk does not have any ground to stand on in his complaint against God. Sure, God's plan to use the Babylonians isn't what Habakkuk wants or would have chosen, but his complaint and subsequent questioning are unfounded. God may be doling out His judgment on His people through the Babylonians, but the Babylonians would eventually face God's punishment and judgment also. Habakkuk just needs to be patient because it will eventually come.

Really, there isn't some hierarchy of wickedness and injustice in the way Habakkuk was implying. All wickedness and injustice will be taken care of by God. It may come in different ways or at different times, but all who advance those things will face God's punishment and judgment. Whether the wickedness and injustice stem from the pride of the Babylonians or from God's own people, God and His justice will reign supreme.

What God accomplished with His use of the Babylonians as a proud person is rather incredible. He simultaneously answered Habakkuk's complaint while also providing a warning for all who would read this later. Yes, the Babylonians were a brutal and powerful people, but they would meet the same fate that every proud person will—downfall and destruction. And if a people like the Babylonians will meet this fate, it should be a warning to all of us about pride.

A Choice

As this chapter comes to a close, I want to draw our attention back to our lives and point out some final things concerning pride. The danger of pride isn't just in making an idol by elevating aspects of our lives such as a job, relationship, or other things of that nature. There is also the danger of us taking our expectations regarding how our lives and the world around us should go and elevating them above God's plans.

Habakkuk once again provides a great example of this. He struggled to understand how and why God would allow what is happening to transpire. Not only that, but when God told him what He was going to do, Habakkuk still struggled with this reality and once again questioned God.

Like Habakkuk, we can struggle to accept what is happening in our lives and the reality around us. Sure, it may be God's will, but it so often isn't part of what we are convinced will make us feel fulfilled, happy, significant, or whole. Again, our pride has us take our expectations concerning how our lives and the world around us should go and wants us to elevate them above God's plans and His will for our lives.

When that happens, we become unhappy with God

because God isn't working within our plans. Even though we know we can't control the future or what happens to us, we are still prideful enough to tell God that what He is doing or how He is working out His plans in the world and our lives is wrong or not good enough.

Think about how prideful that is! That we as part of creation dare approach the Creator with any critique regarding what He is doing and how He is doing it. It is the height of pride and once again found in the original temptation that convinced Adam and Eve they could determine right and wrong.

Finally, if all that wasn't enough, pride can also move our questioning of God from something sincere to something rather sinister. Instead of questioning God as a reaction to what we are seeing and experiencing, our pride can cause us to accuse God of something wrong or sinful.

A look back at Job's story gives us an example of this important line we should never cross. After Job was afflicted and faced a barrage of terrible things, the writer records this:

> In all this Job did not sin or charge God with wrong.
>
> —Job 1:22

Job cries out in anguish and is undoubtedly struggling with what has befallen him, but he never charged God with wrong. That is the key to understanding when we have gone too far in questioning God. It is one thing to not understand and, in our agony and struggles, have it take the form of questioning God; it is a whole different matter to accuse God of wrongdoing.

If Job had accused God of some wrong because of what was happening to him, he would have put himself in the place of judgment over what is right and wrong, usurping God's proper place. Sound familiar? It is pride, and that pride is behind our accusations when we dare to accuse God of any sort of evil or malice. We are not in the place to be able to accuse the God of the universe, so pridefully making accusations, especially ones regarding God's motives or actions being evil, is without question sinful.

All of this and much more highlight the dangers of pride. It is the bedrock sin and arguably the most dangerous. Our pride is so sinful and destructive that God contrasts the proud person with the righteous. God lumps a general lack of uprightness and wickedness all under the umbrella of pride and the proud person. For God to take this position should speak clearly to all of us on the dangers of pride.

What we always need to keep in mind is that the prideful person God talked about generations ago isn't just the Babylonians; it can also be Habakkuk or any one of us. Anybody who elevates themselves or their desires, feelings, thoughts, expectations, or anything else to God's level is the prideful, puffed-up person God was discussing.

Now, I know what the temptation is as you read this. It is to think that, while we all struggle with pride in a sense, you're not that bad. But really, is there a way for us to know if we have fallen to pride's sway in our lives?

The answer is rather simple—follow your worship. What do you adore? What do you give reverence to? What is the thing you couldn't live without? What are you chasing, thinking it will give you ultimate fulfillment? Where do your thoughts and daydreams go naturally? Where do you find your satisfaction? Is it God, or is it something else? Because we know if it isn't God, regardless of what the individual thing we are worshipping may be, we are the proud person who is really worshipping ourselves through our desires, thoughts, expectations, and so on.

We all struggle with pride in one way or another, so it is

extremely easy to succumb to our prideful human nature and move toward idolatry. It is so easy to elevate ourselves to the highest place in our lives when we find ourselves in a situation we don't want to be in or experiencing things that aren't what we want. It doesn't have to lead there, but it often does.

As this chapter ends, I hope we all understand not only what pride is but how truly dangerous it is spiritually. Also, without understanding what God means when He talks about the proud person, we will never fully grasp what God is communicating through the contrast He gives to Habakkuk.

In the next chapter, we will see how God brings everything together and leaves Habakkuk with a choice. It is a critical choice regarding who Habakkuk will decide to be. And as we will see, like Habakkuk, we will also have to choose and answer the question for ourselves—who will we be?

7

FAITH

We were left with a question at the end of the last chapter: Who will you be? It was in reference to the contrast God gave Habakkuk when He responded to his second complaint and questions. Remember, God puts forward this contrast to show that there are really only two types of people when it comes to dealing with difficulties and disappointments.

God started the contrast by talking about the proud person, and He uses the Babylonians as an example of this person. Ultimately, the proud person's pride results in him serving idols.

In the second half of verse four, God gives us a description of the second type of person. With this description, though, we also receive an incredibly important and powerful truth that has reverberated through time.

> Behold, his soul is puffed up; it is not upright within him, but the righteous shall live by his faith.
>
> — Habakkuk 2:4

The righteous shall live by faith. Again, this is such an important and powerful truth that I am sure many, if not most of you, have heard it before. The familiarity with this truth can draw our attention to the verse, but it can also cause us to miss what God is trying to say. Often with extremely popular or well-known verses like this, we can pull them out of their original context in order to slap them on mugs, shirts, or the like. We can become so enamored with them that we lose our understanding of what they are actually communicating. So, let's jump into breaking down what God means when He talks about the righteous person and why He puts righteousness and faith together.

Righteousness

Righteousness simply means to be morally right. When we discuss it biblically, however, it gets a little more complicated depending on the context. For our purposes, righteousness more or less deals with right standing in a relationship. An easy way to understand this would be to think about it more judicially. In any society, there are certain expectations and conduct set out that govern life for all individuals. In the United States, for instance, there are not only specific laws that are to be followed, but there are also basic expectations that people hold regarding how we will interact with each other and the society as a whole.

I ran into this during my travels. I have been blessed to be able to travel the world, and I am always surprised by the various, unwritten customs and practices within different societies and cultures. At times, things I just unconsciously did here in America were not practiced or even unacceptable in other countries. Also, there were various expectations within that society that I was completely oblivious to. Luckily, I never got into any serious trouble, but there were some interesting conversations along the way.

A righteous person would be someone who complied and conformed to the prescribed conduct and expectations held within that society. By contrast, I would not have been considered a righteous person because I did not comply or conform to those rules or expectations.

We use different words to describe these people at different times and at different levels—ethical, law-abiding, upright, corrupt, dishonest, immoral, and so forth—but whatever words we choose, the idea behind it is the same. Someone is either upholding or abandoning the expectations and conduct of a relationship. In this case, it is the relationship between an individual and a society.

Now, all of this is just as applicable to a personal relationship. When thinking about righteousness biblically, the relationship between God and humans takes center stage.

As the one who created all things, God sets the expectations and conduct for our relationship with Him. This is why in the creation narrative, God could command Adam and Eve to not eat the fruit of the tree of the knowledge of good and evil. You can look at that example and think about it any way you like, but as Creator, God is the one who sets the expectations and conduct for us. We may not fully understand or like it, but that really doesn't matter. It is God's prerogative.

This all leads back to what we looked at with the original temptation and sin. The serpent tells Eve and Adam that they can be like God, knowing good and evil. In other words, they wouldn't have to abide by the conduct and expectations that God set out for them. Instead, they could be the ones who determine them. They could determine right and wrong.

Of course, this turned out terribly. Breaking God's command led to sin. If you don't know what I mean when I talk about sin, the biblical idea of sin is multifaceted, but it can be simply thought of as representing humanity's rejection and continued rebellion against God. Again, God set the standard for conduct, but we rebelled against it. Humans "missed the mark" (a common way to think of sin) set for us by God.

While the consequences of sin were dire and far-reaching (affecting all of creation and every human), the greatest consequence of humanity's sin was severing our relationship with God. We were no longer in right relationship with God because He cannot tolerate and be in relationship with sin. It is antithetical to who He is.

So, what we are left with as a result of our sin and our severed relationship with God is the overarching biblical narrative of God's plan to bring humanity back into right relationship with Him. The law, sacrificial system, temple, and so much more are all harbingers of God's unfolding plan to make this happen.

All of this means that when God talks about the righteous, He is talking about those who are in right relationship with Him. This reality leads to some interesting questions in the context of the Old Testament and Habakkuk, however.

If you know how the biblical narrative unfolds, then you know God eventually sent Jesus, His only son, into the world to live a perfect life, die a sacrificial death, and be raised in power from the dead to defeat sin once and for all of time. As a result of Jesus' perfect blood sacrifice and resurrection, all who confess with their mouth that Jesus is Lord and believe in their hearts that God raised Him from the dead will be saved from eternal death (Rom. 10:9) and brought back into right relationship with God.

This is a Christian's salvation and justification (the theological term for the act of God declaring a sinner to now be righteous or in right relationship with Him), and it is beautiful. However, this happened long after Habakkuk questioned God, so how can God talk about the righteous in speaking to Habakkuk when the act that would truly be able to make humans righteous was so far off?

Faith

The answer is found in the truth God revealed to Habakkuk—the righteous will live by faith. If someone is going to be righteous when it comes to God, it will require faith.

While the Bible gives its readers examples of faith more than a straight definition, the writer of Hebrews does give us what seems to be one of the best ways to define biblical faith. He defines faith as the substance of things hoped for and evidence of things not seen (Heb. 11:1). In other words, faith is believing what God has said through His promises and word is true and will happen; it is having such a belief in God's truthfulness to where one aligns their life and actions according to it.

A great example of this is Abraham. God gave Abraham an incredible promise, but it was basically an impossibility. It seemed as though there was no way it would happen. Despite how impossible it was, however, look at what the Bible records as Abraham's response to what God promised:

> And [Abraham] believed the LORD, and he
> counted it to him as righteousness.
>
> — Genesis 15:6

Abraham believed God. Abraham had faith that what God promised would come to pass, and he went forward aligning his life and actions based on that faith. As a result, Abraham's faith was counted to him as righteousness. In other words, Abraham was given right standing with God through his faith in God and His promise.

This is the power of faith in God, His word, and His promises. Even though Abraham never came close to fully understanding what God was planning to accomplish through the promise given to him (Jesus would end up being a descendant of Abraham), he was still declared righteous because he put his faith in God.

This is not only how those before Jesus were declared righteous, but it is how we are declared righteous as well. Scripture is clear that all are saved through faith (Eph. 2:8), so this is what makes the truth given to Habakkuk so incredible. Long before Jesus gave Himself as a sacrifice, God made it clear that the righteous—those who will ultimately find themselves in right relationship with God—will receive that designation and declared status from God as a result of their faith. It won't be what they do or how great they are in human terms. Instead, it will be by faith.

It is not an exaggeration to say the truth given to Habakkuk changed the world. Whether it was through Paul's use of it when writing his New Testament letters or the great reformer Martin Luther who described how this truth changed him, what God said to Habakkuk has effectively shaped history.

The Contrast

. . .

Understanding this timeless truth and why God put righteousness and faith together is one thing, but it is only one part of the bigger picture. As I said before, we have to make sure we don't separate this truth from its context because it was originally given as a response to Habakkuk. It is only one half of the contrast that God was making.

So now that we understand a bit more of what God meant when He talks about the righteous and why He puts it together with faith, the next step is looking at why God chose to make His contrast. Again, God is basically saying there are really only two types of people, the proud and the righteous.

With both pieces of the puzzle, what can we say really separates these two? The answer is found in who or what each person trusts and worships. The proud person is defined by their idolatry while the righteous person by their faith. The proud person trusts in his chosen idols and gives them his worship, while the righteous person trusts in God and gives God his worship.

As we have seen with the proud person, they are their own god. They have elevated themselves and what they believe is right and wrong above God. As a result, they trust in themselves, their determinations, and what they can do. They trust in their abilities, feelings, and desires above anything else. The Babylonians became the perfect example of this. In His description of the Babylonians, God highlights what they trust and who their real god is:

> Then they sweep by like the wind and go on,
> guilty men, whose own might is their god!
>
> — HABAKKUK 1:11

The Babylonians' god is their might. They have elevated

themselves and their ability to conquer nations. They have made an idol of these strengths, and now they trust and worship their own power.

In contrast, God puts forward the righteous person. This individual has the designation of being right with God. Why is he right with God? Because of his faith. He isn't trying to elevate himself and what he can do. It doesn't matter if everything is going the way he wants or if he understands why things are happening to him. Instead, this person trusts God so much that he aligns his life and actions according to God's will and way and not his own. Really, trust becomes a practical outgrowth of his faith in God, His word, and His promises.

With regard to worship, the righteous person does what he was created to do by worshipping God as a response to Him. Whether times are good or bad, his response is worshipping God instead of his elevated understanding, desires, or idea of how things should be going.

These are the two types of people that God lays out in His contrast given to Habakkuk. On the one hand, you have a person who trusts in himself, his desires, and his understanding. On the other, you have a person who trusts in God, His desires, and His understanding. One person's worship goes to idols contrasted against another person whose worship is directed toward God. One is the proud person, while the other is someone who God declares is right with Him.

Fitting It All Together

The differences are stark, but they are important. We cannot forget that this contrast is the heart of this entire book of the

Bible and the key to understanding what God is communicating in His response to Habakkuk.

Now, it's time to fit all the pieces together. If we are going to do that successfully, let's head back to the beginning. Habakkuk questioned God because of the injustice and wickedness that was all around him. He couldn't understand why God was not answering his prayers and intervening to stop what was happening.

God responded by telling Habakkuk that He was not only working all around him, but He was also working in the very things that caused Habakkuk to question Him in the first place. He had a plan to deal with the injustice and wickedness problem, and it involved the Babylonians. God would use them as an instrument of judgment against His own people who had abandoned Him and His way.

Having heard God's plan for dealing with the issues at the heart of his questions, Habakkuk is flabbergasted. How could God use those who were more wicked than His people as an instrument of judgment? That didn't make sense to Habakkuk at all. Wasn't that simply making the original issue worse? Wouldn't that just result in more injustice and wickedness? What about the Babylonians? Are they just getting off scot-free? If God is punishing His own people for wickedness and injustice, why aren't the Babylonians getting punished? These are all things Habakkuk either verbalized or implied in his response to God's plan. He is so taken aback by what God said that he actually went as far as to challenge God to answer him.

With this in mind, you begin to see why God answers Habakkuk differently with His second response. God gave Habakkuk a promise that He is working and doing something that he wouldn't believe even if he was told, but that didn't assuage Habakkuk at all. In fact, as we know, Habakkuk is so worked up he is challenging God.

With this newest response, God doesn't just give Habakkuk an answer as He did the first time. Instead, while God will address the heart of the issue Habakkuk brings before Him, this response is rather unexpected—God actually responds to Habakkuk's challenge with a challenge of His own.

Now, you may be wondering, "When did God challenge Habakkuk?" And the answer comes from the contrast we have been looking at. The challenge is what God is communicating to Habakkuk when He gives him the contrast. This is the reason why the contrast is the heart of Habakkuk's book.

Responding to Habakkuk's challenge with a challenge can seem like a strange way for God to respond, but it isn't the first time that God has done something like this. I have referenced Job previously, but God's response to Job shows some similarities to the response He gives to Habakkuk. As we saw earlier, Job wanted to question God regarding the things that happened to him. He wanted to make a case for his innocence. Well, God does eventually show up on the scene, and look at how He responds:

> [1] Then the LORD answered Job out of the whirlwind and said: [2] "Who is this that darkens counsel by words without knowledge? [3] Dress for action like a man; I will question you, and you make it known to me.
>
> —Job 38:1–3

God turns things around on Job. Job desired to question God, but God shows up and questions him instead. Similarly, Habakkuk challenges God, so God challenges Habakkuk.

In order to challenge Habakkuk, God would again reveal

something to him. God's first response filled Habakkuk in on how He would take care of the injustice and wickedness problem. Now, in His newest response, God reveals to Habakkuk the reality the Babylonians would face. Though the Babylonians were a great and powerful people, they would be brought low and shamed. They would not escape God's heavy hand of judgment.

So, Habakkuk's issue with God using the Babylonians as His instrument of judgment against His own people shouldn't have been an issue at all. Again, Habakkuk was convinced that doing this would just result in more injustice and wickedness, but God shows it doesn't matter. God will punish all those who are wicked, which includes proud people like the Babylonians. None will escape His righteous judgment. It doesn't matter if they are a great nation or His own people; God's judgment against sin, injustice, and wickedness will happen.

With this revealed, it shouldn't make any difference how God chooses to go about doling out His judgment. Whether God's people are judged first or even if He uses a people against them who are more wicked than they are, He accomplishes His purpose—the result is ultimately the same. The wicked will all eventually face judgment.

Do you see how it is all coming together? Instead of responding the way He did before, God gives Habakkuk a vision of what will happen, and it starts with the fact that Habakkuk needs to be patient. God has a plan for Habakkuk's issues, including the one regarding His use of the Babylonians against His own people. Habakkuk needs to wait on God because the Babylonian's end (and the end of all who are wicked) is sure.

Habakkuk and all who would hear this vision need to remember that God's word is always true. It will surely come to pass and not be a lie. Even if Habakkuk doesn't see it, even if he doesn't understand it, even if it isn't the way he wants or the timing he would choose, he has to remember who God is, that He has a plan, and it is all moving to the end that God has determined.

The Challenge

Now, this is, in essence, how God challenges Habakkuk. In light of all God has revealed to him in both responses, Habakkuk has a choice. He can choose to be one of two people through how he will respond to all God has revealed, the proud person or the righteous person.

God set it all up through the contrast and subsequent revelation, and now the ball was back in Habakkuk's court. He has the truth that God gave him, and he has the assurance that God has a plan for everything, including the Babylonians. So, how will he respond? Will he be the proud person or the righteous one?

On the one hand, he can continue to complain to and question God. He can continue down the path he has been traveling and persist in challenging and fighting against God and His plans. But if Habakkuk makes that choice after all God has said, Habakkuk would choose to be the prideful person.

Basically, Habakkuk would be making an idol out of his beliefs. He would be elevating how he thinks everything should be going over the sovereign plan of God. He would be placing his trust in himself and his understanding.

It was undoubtedly tough for Habakkuk to stand by and watch all the injustice and wickedness among God's people. And hearing how God would judge them through the Babylonians could have only made it worse. However, God has responded twice to his questioning and revealed some amazing things. So the question remains, what will he do?

As I said, he can certainly continue to go down the path he has been traveling by pridefully digging his heels in by rejecting God and His plan, but it will not end well. He will be the proud person, and as God made abundantly clear, it will lead to the same result as the people he despises so much—the Babylonians.

On the other hand, in light of the reality that God will also judge and punish the Babylonians, Habakkuk can choose to be the righteous person who lives by faith. Everything that is happening is just as tough for the righteous person as it is for the proud person. Things are also not happening the way he wants them to, but this person reacts differently than his counterpart. The righteous person trusts God when He says that He will take care of everything. Again, even though it isn't happening how or when he wants it, this person chooses to have faith in God and trust Him.

Habakkuk needs to choose. Will he trust God or himself? Will he trust God's word, or will he trust in his own understanding of the situation? Will he elevate himself like the proud person by "worshiping" his own thoughts regarding how things should go, or will he respond to God in worship like the righteous person over and above what he wants or understands?

This is how it all comes together. This is why the contrast was so important. Through His response, God turned things back around on Habakkuk. This whole time, Habakkuk had the spotlight on God. He had been the one questioning and complaining to God. He had been the one challenging God.

God in His loving grace responded to all of Habakkuk's questions and complaints. He even responded to the challenge that Habakkuk brought to Him. Now, God puts the spotlight on Habakkuk. He challenges Habakkuk to make a choice. Who will he be? The proud person or the righteous one.

Who Will We Be?

For us, the same question could be asked. Will we be the person who worships and puts their trust in themselves, or will we be the person who trusts and worships God? Will we be the proud person or the righteous person?

As we have seen, if we are going to be righteous—just and in right relationship with God—we will have to live by faith. There is no other path. Our lives will exude faith in all aspects of it. That is why the writer of Hebrews states that it is impossible to please God without faith (Heb. 11:6). So to be that individual who is in right relationship with God, we will be living a life defined by faith.

As you read that, I am sure it may be a very daunting proposition, especially when you look at your life. Many, if not most of us, would say that we aren't living a life of faith as we should. Maybe you would describe your life as being one that hardly exudes faith. In fact, maybe as you read this, you find yourself in the proud person camp much more than the righteous one. It can even be discouraging to look at how we live and wonder if we can make the necessary changes to really live by faith. At times and in some areas of our lives, it can perhaps seem impossible.

If you are at that place or anywhere close, the good news is that it is far from impossible. No one is saying it will be easy, but if we make the choice to have our lives defined by faith instead of all the other things we usually chase, we will join a long list of others who came before us. Like theirs, our lives can also be defined by faith instead of comfort, fear, or needing things to go our way. We can look at their example and be committed to having that level of faith.

Like Abraham, if called to go somewhere, even if we don't know exactly where we are going, we can still trust God and go. Like Joseph, even if everything goes wrong, we can still know that what was meant for evil, God can use for good. Like Moses, if called to something we can't do on our own, we can have faith that God will go before us.

Like the Israelites marching around Jericho, if God tells us to do something we don't understand or that doesn't make sense, we can choose to do it anyway. Like Hannah, even if something is absolutely impossible, we can pray in faith knowing our God is the God of the impossible.

Like Shadrach, Meshach, and Abednego, even if the cost of following God is high, we can refuse to bow down to anything else, knowing our God can save us. And like Elijah standing against the prophets of Baal, even if we are outnumbered or alone, we can stand confidently in faith knowing God is the true God, and if He is all we have, we have everything we need on our side.

I could go on and on, but the testimony of all these individuals and so many more demonstrate the power of faith being lived out. This is exactly what God is looking for from those who follow Him. If we follow the examples left for us, we can also be the righteous person, living a life defined by faith.

Sure, if we choose to walk in faith, there will be tough times and moments where we want to throw our hands up and question God regarding why and how He is doing things. That is where a prophet like Habakkuk found himself, and that is the place so many Christians throughout time found themselves. However, we have the same truth and choice that were given to Habakkuk generations ago.

We can choose to continue railing against God and how He

is working. We can pridefully dig into our position that things don't make sense and shouldn't be this way. We can even attempt to elevate ourselves to God's level by deciding that we want to be the ones who control our lives and destiny.

Or, even though we may feel all those things and more—even though everything within us may want to move that direction—we can instead choose to have faith in God by trusting in His word and the promises He revealed. Instead of responding with questioning and complaining, we can commit to worshipping God even in the midst of our worst moments and most difficult times, knowing that is how we were created to respond to Him.

We weren't created to worship anything else. We weren't created to be our own gods trying to make our own ways work. We were created to glorify God and—even when we don't understand why things are happening or how it will ever result in anything that could be considered good—worship Him because we know He is worthy of it.

Again, it isn't easy when we are in those tough moments. It is difficult when we find ourselves in situations like Habakkuk. But for anyone reading these words who considers themselves a follower of God, we have something that Habakkuk and his original readers never dreamed or imagined—the knowledge of what Jesus did.

We know the sacrifice that God made for us and how His love was demonstrated brutally and gloriously on the cross. We know that nothing could ever separate us from the love of God as a result (Rom. 8:35–39). So how could we fail to worship God even in the middle of our darkest moments?

When we are facing the toughest of circumstances, let us choose to live by faith and not by sight. And in the midst of it, let us choose to worship God even if all we have is the cross and empty grave. Because if that is all we have, that is more than enough for us to give God the worship He deserves.

Let's look at God's challenge to Habakkuk and take the question seriously for our lives. Who will we be? Will we be the proud person or the righteous one? Will we chase our idols or live by faith?

Only you can answer.

8
PRAYER

If there is something we all understand, it is that our choices make a difference. What we choose can have a tremendous effect on our lives and how we are remembered.

Have you ever made a choice that had that type of effect? I know I have many times. One such choice centered on what I was going to do for my career. Originally, I was planning to be an attorney, but through a series of events, I moved into ministry. Looking back, I can definitely see God's hand on what transpired, but I sometimes wonder what would have happened if I had stuck with my original plans. How would my life look now? How different would things be? Eventually, when my life is over, will I be remembered differently because of this choice and others like it?

That last question is one that particularly hangs over my head at times. How does this choice or that choice affect how I will be remembered? Now, I don't want this to sound like a prideful question because it isn't meant to be. Instead, it is a way to pull myself out of any particular moment and gain some much-needed perspective.

I have made plenty of decisions emotionally or without

much thought. Most of the time, it doesn't end as well as I would hope. On at least a few occasions, things ended extremely poorly, to say the least. So, this question helps me when I need a thirty-thousand-foot view on important decisions. It helps me understand if I am acting too emotionally or just reacting in a negative way. Also, it can help give me a long-term view rather than making a decision where I am just caught in the moment.

I have always believed there are never really any neutral decisions. One way or another, each and every decision will affect our lives either positively or negatively. Some of these decisions can and will define us, so it is always important to try to be careful when making those types of decisions.

In a way, Habakkuk is faced with a defining decision. Amazingly, he had the privilege of interacting with God and getting his questions and complaints addressed. Now, he has a decision to make regarding God's challenge over who he will be. Will he be the proud person who trusts himself and elevates his own thoughts of how things should go, or will he be like the righteous person who has faith in God and trusts God over and above what he wants or understands?

With the ball now in Habakkuk's court, he has a tremendous response:

> [1] A prayer of Habakkuk the prophet, according to Shigionoth. [2] O LORD, I have heard the report of you, and your work, O LORD, do I fear. In the midst of the years revive it; in the midst of the years make it known; in wrath remember mercy.
>
> — HABAKKUK 3:1–2

Habakkuk prays. His response is to go to God in prayer.

Now, for clarification, any time we communicate with God it is technically considered prayer, so that means Habakkuk has been praying the whole time if you want to think of it that way. However, this prayer is different than everything else that came before it. This falls in line with what we all typically think when we think of prayer. It is also specifically introduced as a prayer. For this reason, the final chapter in this biblical book is markedly different than the others. No longer is Habakkuk having a back-and-forth with God. Now, Habakkuk begins to take a different posture than he had previously.

What is noteworthy about this prayer is that it is recorded for us in the form of a psalm. The reason this is significant is it means Habakkuk's prayer eventually spread and was more than likely sung ("To the choirmaster: with stringed instruments" [Hab. 3:19]). Needless to say, this prayer of Habakkuk was a powerful one that went on to affect generations of listeners. But what makes this prayer so special? Why did it eventually spread to others? I believe the reason is due to what this prayer communicates as it progresses.

Habakkuk's Prayer

The prayer starts with a plea to God, as seen in verse two. Habakkuk asks God to repeat the great works of deliverance He had done previously again in his day. Now, this may seem strange until you understand the context of it.

While the plea is the first part of his prayer, Habakkuk actually introduces his plea in a very specific way—with a recognition of the greatness and power of God. Habakkuk tells God that he knows of His greatness and how it has been demonstrated clearly by the powerful works He's done in the past.

Without mentioning it explicitly at this point, the Exodus would seem to be on his mind when he says this to God. It was a defining moment for God's people, and there may not have been a greater example that demonstrates the greatness of God than those moments of deliverance for His people (e.g., the plagues against Egypt, parting the Red Sea, destruction of the Egyptian army). Recognizing that power, Habakkuk tells God how in awe of Him he is. Habakkuk can't help but have the fear of the Lord that results in an absolute reverence for Him and His greatness.

After beginning with this focus on God's great power and, specifically, His power to deliver, Habakkuk brings his request before God. By asking God to repeat His great works of deliverance again in his day, Habakkuk is, in essence, asking God to deliver His people from the coming invasion of the Babylonians just as He previously delivered His people during the Exodus from Egypt.

This is a rather bold request, especially when you consider that Habakkuk knows God's people are the reason for the rampant wickedness and injustice. They are the reason God is using the Babylonians as His instrument of judgment. Habakkuk is basically praying God would deliver His people from the fate they rightfully deserve.

He is praying this, however, because he knows the Babylonians are going to crush and destroy the people of Judah. They stand no chance against a foe like the Babylonians, so Habakkuk is pleading with God for Him to deliver the people of Judah by sparing them from this foe. As the end of verse two makes clear, even though they are guilty, Habakkuk is still looking for God to show mercy even in the middle of His wrath.

What is happening here is striking. Habakkuk is obviously still extremely bothered and struggling with God's plan to use the Babylonians. Yes, he has received God's response and knows God will take care of the Babylonians eventually, but Habakkuk hopes it will happen now. He is making one more appeal for God to save His people.

The reason I am really drilling down on this is I believe Habakkuk shows us a very human reaction here. Even with the promise given earlier and subsequent truth that made it clear God will deal with the Babylonians, Habakkuk is still praying for his people. He is still going before God and pleading that He would show His greatness again in this situation by delivering His people from the coming invasion.

As I read this verse, it strikes me as something quite common and frankly human. I think we have all been in Habakkuk's position at one time or another. Maybe what we were praying for seemed impossible or the matter decided. Maybe we were told it is the end of the line in some way. What do so many of us do in those situations? We still pray; we still cry out to God, hoping that our prayers will change things.

Why do we do this? Why as Christians do we continue to pray and plead with God to change our circumstances or outcomes when it has basically been decided? Well, like Habakkuk, we know God is great and powerful. We know He is the God who can do things that seem impossible, so we cry out seeking for Him to change our situation. We continue to go to God in prayer, knowing He is great enough to change any situation regardless of how final the outcome appears to be.

This is such a beautiful aspect of prayer—the power of prayer. Anyone who knows me knows I believe in the power of prayer, and I think Habakkuk demonstrates this power clearly. Even though God said the Babylonian invasion would happen, guess what? Habakkuk is still praying. He knows prayer can change things, and this plea appears to show that he will keep praying even to the end.

I really think this one verse could minister to a lot of people on its own. Whatever you are facing, no matter how dire or hopeless it seems, keep praying. If Habakkuk received confirmation directly from God Himself that something would happen yet still continues to pray for things to be changed, I think we should follow his example by continuing to pray for God to work in everything we face. Like Habakkuk, let's be convinced of the power of God. Let's never stop praying regardless of how determined the outcome seems.

Glorifying God

While Habakkuk's prayer starts with this plea for God to deliver His people again, it does not stop there. Habakkuk's prayer continues by keeping its focus on the greatness and power of God.

In the next part of his prayer, Habakkuk moves his focus from requesting something of God to glorifying Him instead. Through the majority of the verses that are left in the chapter, Habakkuk looks back on what God has done by again making the Exodus part of his focus. Over and over, Habakkuk marvels at God's power and greatness as it was demonstrated in the deliverance of His people.

Eventually, Habakkuk makes an important transition. While he continues to talk about what God has done, he also begins to focus on who God is. In verse thirteen, Habakkuk switches from simply emphasizing God's power in light of His actions. Now, he begins to highlight God's power by portraying Him as a mighty warrior who is ready for battle.

> You went out for the salvation of your people,
> for the salvation of your anointed. You

> crushed the head of the house of the wicked,
> laying him bare from thigh to neck.
>
> — Habakkuk 3:13

The reason I am specifically highlighting this verse is that I believe it clearly signals a change in Habakkuk. Throughout the entire book to this point, Habakkuk has been complaining and questioning God. Now, Habakkuk's questions have turned into statements like the one above. Habakkuk moved from wondering how God could possibly use a people like the Babylonians against His own people to proclaiming the greatness of God by portraying Him as a warrior who crushes His enemies. That is quite a change. Habakkuk's move from challenging God to glorifying Him represents a stark shift, and it begins to signal something important.

Throughout this section of the prayer, Habakkuk connects what God *has done* for His people with what Habakkuk is confident God *will do* for His people. In order to understand what I mean by that, look again at how Habakkuk is describing God.

Previously, like a great warrior, God went out and defeated the enemies of His people. God secured their salvation and saved them even when they faced terrible and powerful enemies like the Egyptians. During that time and others, God demonstrated His love for His people by crushing their enemies. It didn't matter who the enemy was or how mighty they were, time and time again, God would go before His people and mightily save them.

Now, faced with what seems like the inevitable destruction of his people at the hands of the Babylonians, Habakkuk is demonstrating his faith in God by praying and believing God will once again save His people. Sure, Habakkuk made it clear through the plea that started his prayer what he would prefer (that God would stop the Babylonians from invading in the first place), but even if God doesn't answer his plea and save His people that way, Habakkuk will continue to glorify God because he is convinced God will still somehow save His people as He has done so many times before.

Declaration of Faith

Everything Habakkuk has been praying comes together as his prayer draws to a close. His plea, his glorifying of God's power and greatness, and his faith coalesce beautifully in verse sixteen.

> I hear, and my body trembles; my lips quiver at the sound; rottenness enters into my bones; my legs tremble beneath me. Yet I will quietly wait for the day of trouble to come upon people who invade us.
>
> — Habakkuk 3:16

In this verse, Habakkuk gives an incredible declaration of faith, and it is made more potent by everything that proceeded it. To this point, Habakkuk proclaimed the power and greatness of God. He glorified God and declared that God can save His people again just as He did before.

But now, Habakkuk makes it clear that he has also heard what God said to him through His responses—the Babylonians will invade. As we have seen, Habakkuk is still praying for a different outcome, but Habakkuk is also not going to pretend what God has clearly revealed regarding the fate of His people isn't the reality they are facing. So even though Habakkuk knows the power of prayer and is full of faith that God can save His people again, Habakkuk won't ignore what God has made plain to him.

In verse sixteen, Habakkuk is explaining the visceral reaction he has as he thinks about what is to come. The imagery of his body shaking, including legs trembling, lips quivering, and the feeling of rottenness spreading throughout his body, are all harsh images. Taken together, it shows Habakkuk is also full of dread and fear over what God said will happen to His people.

As you read this, it may not seem like much of a declaration of faith. As a matter of fact, if many Christians talked about what they were facing that way, most would assume they didn't have much faith. But Habakkuk's declaration didn't end there. He goes on to say that, despite what he thinks and how it makes him feel, he will remain quiet and wait on God. He will ultimately submit to God's will if that is what God has decided.

What a declaration! As I read it, I feel my spirit lifted by this prophet's words. Habakkuk made it absolutely clear how bothered he is by everything. From the beginning to the end of his prayer, there is no denying it. He started his prayer by pleading for God to change His mind, and it continued throughout the majority of it. But Habakkuk ends his prayer by trusting God enough to accept whatever He decides, even if it results in the invasion and destruction of his people.

This reminds me of one of my favorite statements of faith in the Bible—the one made by Shadrach, Meshach, and Abednego. After they wouldn't bow down and worship the golden image set up by Nebuchadnezzar, he threatened to throw them into a fiery furnace. Look at how they responded:

> [16] Shadrach, Meshach, and Abednego answered
> and said to the king, "O Nebuchadnezzar,
> we have no need to answer you in this

> matter. ¹⁷ If this be so, our God whom we serve is able to deliver us from the burning fiery furnace, and he will deliver us out of your hand, O king. ¹⁸ But if not, be it known to you, O king, that we will not serve your gods or worship the golden image that you have set up."
>
> — DANIEL 3:16–18

They basically say, "Our God can and will deliver us, but regardless of what He chooses, we will remain faithful to Him." This is such an amazing statement of faith, and Habakkuk's statement is rather similar. Habakkuk made it known that God can deliver the people of Judah from the Babylonians, and he is specifically praying for it. But even if God doesn't answer his prayer, Habakkuk also knows God is powerful and great enough to still save His people, whether it happens the way he wants or not.

Again, Habakkuk knows God can save His people because He has been proclaiming God's power and greatness throughout his prayer. God has done it before, and Habakkuk is sure God will do it again one way or another. So against that backdrop, Habakkuk says he will stop questioning and go forward quietly waiting. He will continue to believe in faith that somehow and someway God will again save His people despite the coming invasion.

Habakkuk's Decision

. . .

To say Habakkuk is in a different place than he was before may be an understatement. Sure, everything is still tough and not how he wants it to be, but he is making the decision to respond differently than he did previously. He is choosing faith.

Really, through this declaration of faith, Habakkuk is responding to God's challenge concerning who he was going to be. In light of all that transpired and will happen, Habakkuk could have chosen to be the proud person, but Habakkuk is making it clear he has decided to take the righteous path.

To this point, Habakkuk has done a lot of questioning and complaining. In his disillusionment, he even challenged God to respond to him, but Habakkuk makes it clear that he will now hold his tongue. Instead of more questioning and complaining, he will hold on to what God promised. He will quietly wait on God.

Habakkuk is choosing to move forward in faith by trusting what God has said is true and will come to pass. As he said in verse sixteen, he will wait for the day the Babylonians face their judgment. Habakkuk is choosing the path of the righteous even though the outcome isn't what he wants. He has decided to trust God and live by faith.

Through his prayer and declaration of faith, Habakkuk becomes an example for all of us. He becomes the embodiment of the truth God revealed in saying the righteous will live by faith, and his journey to this point illustrates it beautifully.

Really, there isn't much that has gone Habakkuk's way. His prayers seem to keep going unanswered, he is going through a horrible time with all the rampant injustice and wickedness around him, and even the future looks bleak at best because he knows the Babylonians are going to invade, basically destroying his people and land. No one could blame Habakkuk for reacting negatively to all of this. For some people reading his book, it might seem reasonable for Habakkuk to want to give up, continue to question God, or maybe even get to the point of losing his belief in this God who revealed Himself to him. I mean, if most of us were in Habakkuk's place, how many people do you think would react that way? Or, at the very least, how many people do you think would question how a God who claims to be good and all-powerful could allow what is happening and will happen to transpire?

Instead, what does Habakkuk do? He chooses the path of faith and trusting God. Again, nothing is easy and how he wants it to be, but he will move forward in faith. He will wait on God's plan and purposes to work themselves out.

Our Prayer

Habakkuk becomes this incredible example for us, but as we have seen, it wasn't easy. And I am sure many of us can relate to that lack of ease. If you are a Christian, you know (or now hopefully know) the importance of faith, but what does it mean for your immediate situation or circumstances? Maybe you currently are or have been where Habakkuk found himself—nothing seems to be going your way, everything is falling apart, your prayers aren't getting answered, and the future doesn't look particularly bright.

What are we supposed to do when we find ourselves there? Hopefully, like Habakkuk, we all choose to live by faith, but is there some next step that will help us navigate through what we are facing? The answer is yes, and I believe we have already seen what is arguably the most important aspect of it—prayer.

Even near the end of his story, Habakkuk is still praying and calling out for God to change things, so we absolutely should be following Habakkuk's example by continuing to pray. He continues to pray even though the outcome seems sure because he knows the power of prayer and the power of the one he is praying to. God is the God of the impossible, so Habakkuk has not given up that his prayers can potentially change things.

This is why Habakkuk keeps going back to God's power and might. In his prayer, Habakkuk is constantly bringing his attention back to who God is and what He can do. So even with a prayer that seems impossible or unlikely, Habakkuk knows God can still do it.

Now, this next part is also important, so don't miss it. If you have been in church for any amount of time, you probably see and hear a lot about prayer and faith, right? I'm sure you have heard great sermons or read engaging books revolving around things such as mountains moving and dead bones coming to life.

To clarify, I am in no way hating on sermons or books that talk about these miracles or others. I think they are incredible displays of God's power. These and every other example of God's power should move us to be filled with awe at how mighty our God really is. And then that should lead us to pray in faith for the impossible or pray for God to intervene powerfully in our lives.

We should all pray that way! However, don't miss what Habakkuk also prays in verse sixteen. It not only stands as a declaration of his faith, but it is also a statement signifying his submission to God's will. If you want to think of it another way, think of verse sixteen as Habakkuk's way of praying what Jesus prayed in Gethsemane before His crucifixion, "Not my will, but yours be done" (Matt. 26:39, Mk. 14:36, Lk. 22:42).

Habakkuk doesn't want anything that is coming (and we know he is praying against it), but he tells God he will wait for the coming invasion and the eventual downfall of the Babylonians. In other words, Habakkuk wants God to change things, but he will submit to God's will over and above what he wants. He even goes as far as to say that he will wait quietly for it.

The reason I am pointing this out is simple. When many of us pray, we pray selfishly. We pray believing God can and will do amazing things, but so often what we are doing when we pray these prayers is trying to get our will done instead of wanting to see God's will done. And I know there are so many Christians who say you aren't praying a prayer of faith if you don't name it and claim it, claim the victory, believe completely knowing you will absolutely get what you are asking for, or any other version of those ideas. I don't know how many times over the years I have heard this sort of sentiment in one form or another.

But to those who hold this line of reasoning, I'll just point back to Habakkuk. Habakkuk is praying that God will stop the invasion. He is praying that God will intervene, and he knows God can do it! He has complete belief and faith that God can answer his prayers and deliver His people because God has done it before. Habakkuk's prayer is full of him constantly declaring God's power and might! But Habakkuk still ends his prayer by saying he will wait quietly for the day of trouble. Even after all his statements regarding the power and might of God, Habakkuk chooses to land in a place of acceptance regarding the will of God for his life and circumstances.

Do you see how powerful that is? So many pastors and preachers today would say that Habakkuk is not really believing. They would declare that Habakkuk isn't praying a prayer of faith because of his last statement. I am sure some would say he isn't praying a prayer of faith because he is clearly doubting that God will answer his prayer. What is actually happening, however, is the exact opposite!

To be clear, the Bible does say we should pray without doubting (Jas. 1:6, Matt. 21:21, Mk. 11:22–23), but that does not mean what so many take it to mean. Again, Habakkuk provides a perfect example of what a true prayer of faith with submission to God looks like.

Habakkuk is praying and knows God can stop what is coming, but it is *because* of his faith and his decision to live by faith that he will submit to God's will whether he likes it or not. His faith isn't tied to getting the answer he wants. Instead, his faith is fully with the God who has shown Himself faithful time and time again. He may not like what it is, but Habakkuk resolves to faithfully submit to God's will over and above what he would choose or want.

As I said earlier, if you are at a place similar to where Habakkuk finds himself—where it seems like everything is going wrong and there isn't a great future before you—pray and keep praying. Pray for God to intervene and work powerfully in your life and all around you. Absolutely do it and know that God can do great things and even work miraculously in your life, just like He has done throughout the Bible!

But don't think it stops there. Don't think living by faith stops at just declaring God's power and believing what you want will happen. It also means bringing yourself to a place of submission. It means bringing yourself to the place where you can honestly say and mean it, "God, your will be done." Or, "God, I may not want it this way or even understand why this is happening, but I know you are a good God who is doing something through this that I wouldn't believe even if I was told. So I will wait on you."

That is truly living by faith. It isn't just accepting good times and good things, but it is also being able to submit to God, knowing that His will and way are always best whether we like the outcome or not.

Let's follow Habakkuk's example. This prayer that ministered to countless others as a psalm is one of *submission*. Sure, there are massive statements centered on God's power and might (along with his declaration of faith that answered God's challenge), but it all falls under the umbrella of submission. As with Habakkuk, let's make sure we are submitting to God and His will.

Live by faith and pray. Pray a lot and all of the time. Let's believe God for great things! As we do that, though, let's also position ourselves in a posture of humble submission as we wait on God and His will to ultimately be done, knowing that He loves us and is working it all out for our good and His glory.

9

WORSHIP

The end can be a tricky thing. There are times when endings can be great, while other times it is anything but that. The ending of a great book or show has to be one of the more difficult things to accomplish. I don't know how many times I have followed a show just to be disappointed by the ending, and I am sure I am not alone. As a matter of fact, I bet there are many of you who had something pop into your mind as you were reading about disappointing endings. And what unfortunately happens is that a lackluster ending can spoil the entire show or book.

If you were trying to write a great ending for Habakkuk's journey, it would seem as though Habakkuk's prayer of submission would be a perfect place to end his book. Habakkuk had been struggling with God's plan and what He was doing the entire time, but by the end, he has finally come to a place where he is ready to submit to God's will and way. The prophet who was questioning, complaining, and even challenging God has said he will remain quiet while trusting in God's will and plan.

Again, that seems like a great place for the story to end, right? You may be sitting there wondering what else there is to do? Habakkuk made the turn to moving forward by faith, so what else needs to be accomplished? This seems like the best ending one could hope for considering everything that has been going on.

The reality is, however, that Habakkuk's story does not end there. Instead, there are a few more verses that shouldn't be overlooked. In a way, these verses elevate this biblical book and Habakkuk's story to something truly memorable. In my opinion, it takes the ending from great to perfect, and I say that because I believe something rather unbelievable is demonstrated. Look at what Habakkuk does next and how it all ends:

> [17] Though the fig tree should not blossom, nor fruit be on the vines, the produce of the olive fail and the fields yield no food, the flock be cut off from the fold and there be no herd in the stalls, [18] yet I will rejoice in the LORD; I will take joy in the God of my salvation. [19] GOD, the Lord, is my strength; he makes my feet like the deer's; he makes me tread on my high places.
>
> — HABAKKUK 3:17–19

It all ends with worship. Out of everything we could have been left with, we are left with Habakkuk worshipping. With what has transpired, this may seem unexpected, but really, it is a beautiful and important response.

Now, I do want to clarify that these few verses shouldn't be separated from Habakkuk's prayer that was discussed in the last chapter. As a matter of fact, these verses are a continuation of the prayer and psalm Habakkuk is giving to God. While it certainly all fits and flows together, I am drawing a distinction here because I see this as another important shift in Habakkuk.

The story could have just ended with him committing to live faithfully by waiting quietly as a result of his trust in God. Instead, as we have seen, Habakkuk's story ends with worship.

You see, Habakkuk may be committing to remain quiet with regard to his questions and complaints, but he is making it abundantly clear that he will not remain quiet when it comes to his worship of God. Habakkuk has glorified God and honored Him throughout the prayer, but now he changes his posture once again from one of submission to one of worship. This is a beautiful thing, and it overflows with value and meaning for the reader.

Really, one aspect of this change toward worship I find interesting is that Habakkuk's circumstances haven't really changed at all. Habakkuk may be changing, but nothing around him is. From the very beginning until now, Habakkuk is still pretty much in the same place. He is still surrounded by injustice and wickedness, his prayers aren't being answered, and he now knows about the coming invasion of his people. Actually, if you include the knowledge of the upcoming invasion, it could be argued that Habakkuk may be in an even worse place now compared to where he was at the beginning. So how Habakkuk is reacting at the end of his book is rather incredible. It is one thing to, in faith, go forward submitting to God by accepting what is happening or will happen. It is another thing altogether to start worshipping in the middle of it.

There are many followers of God who may be able to make declarations of faith and submit to God's will during difficult times, but to go even further by responding in worship seems like a lot. That is exactly how Habakkuk responds, though.

. . .

Don't Ignore the Problem

> Though the fig tree should not blossom, nor fruit be on the vines, the produce of the olive fail and the fields yield no food, the flock be cut off from the fold and there be no herd in the stalls,
>
> — Habakkuk 3:17

Look at how Habakkuk starts his worship in verse seventeen. Habakkuk speaks in terms of the upcoming invasion by the Babylonians and the inevitable aftermath. As you could have probably guessed, the description is not great. Habakkuk knows the losses will be immense. He knows there will be devastation and destruction after the invasion. The land will be ruined and the Babylonians will take whatever they want from whatever is left. Even basic things such as food will be scarce in the aftermath. The people who remain will be left with little more than devastation.

Quite the rosy picture, right? However, this is where Habakkuk actually starts his worship, and the fact he starts here is significant. It seems as though Habakkuk is saying that, in spite of all that is coming, in spite of how terrible and destructive it will be, in spite of all of that and more, he will still worship. This of course doesn't mean he is going to be happy or OK with it all, but none of it will stop him from worshipping. For Habakkuk, it doesn't matter how bad it gets—he will still rejoice. This sentiment seems almost out of place considering what he is describing. It will be absolutely terrible. Even still, Habakkuk says he will worship.

I don't know if you had the same reaction as I did when I

read this, but I thought it was powerful. It's as if Habakkuk is staring down the barrel of a gun that will result in the destruction of the people and land he loves, but he is declaring his worship will not stop.

What makes this response so striking is it's almost the exact opposite of the one so many Christians have nowadays. Most if not all Christians know worship is important, and along with that, there is the understanding that God deserves our worship. Yet, despite knowing all of this, a response like Habakkuk's is often the exception and not the rule. We know we should worship and that God is worthy of it, but Christians still struggle to worship Him during difficult times and seasons. Why is this the case, and how do we worship when times are tough? How do we worship when we naturally don't want to? There may not be a silver bullet that covers every situation, but I do think Habakkuk's story gives us a great example of how we can get there.

During my years of ministry, I have not only seen this question regarding worship come into play in many Christian's lives, but I have also wrestled with it. It isn't simple by any means. The thought of worshipping in the middle of our difficulty can seem foreign when we are walking through it. During those times, worshipping can be the furthest thing from our minds.

What we are often left with is a tension. We know worship is important, and we know we need to do it. But we certainly don't feel like doing it. Unfortunately, what ends up happening is so many Christians falter under the weight of their circumstances and accept a faulty belief we assume will help us worship God during those dark times. The belief is that you need to ignore the bad things happening in your life. The sense is you just need to forget about the bad things—almost compartmentalize it and put it away—if you are ever going to be able to worship God during those difficult times.

However, what Habakkuk shows us is completely different. He is specifically saying he will not blindly ignore what is happening around him. He is absolutely aware of the current situation (rampant injustice and wickedness), the coming invasion, and the destruction it will cause. He doesn't shy away from it at all. As a matter of fact, Habakkuk is actually making it a part of his worship!

As he continues, the reader sees why Habakkuk decides to implement it in his worship. Habakkuk's aim isn't simply to get through the difficulty; it isn't just to check a box because he knows he should worship. As we saw, even though what he fears and has been praying against appears as though it will become a reality, it will not be a deterrent to his worship of the Lord.

Habakkuk doesn't want to stop there, though; he actually goes even further. Not only will he keep worshipping, but he goes on to say he will also have joy in the middle of what he is facing:

> Yet I will rejoice in the LORD; I will take joy in the God of my salvation.
>
> — Habakkuk 3:18

Through these verses, Habakkuk shows use that ignoring our issues or difficulties isn't the way we should worship when times are tough and we aren't inclined to. Even with this in mind, there still feels like something is missing. Simply refusing to ignore the problem can't be all there is to the answer, right? I mean, again, how can anyone continue to worship God and even have joy right in the midst of all life's difficulties like Habakkuk was able to do? There has to be something else.

Well, there is, and Habakkuk shows us what it is and why it

is significant. Diving a little deeper gives us the why behind how Habakkuk is able to worship.

An Opportunity for God

We already know from the last chapter that his focus is on God and His power, but Habakkuk now shows us a subtle change that really is the linchpin behind his joy and worship. This change is seen through Habakkuk's statement regarding how he will take joy in "the God of my salvation."

As discussed in the last chapter, Habakkuk is very aware of God's work of salvation with His people in the past. He saved His people over and over again, and as we saw in his prayer, Habakkuk is convinced God can and will do it again. In other words, what God has done previously gives Habakkuk hope in the present despite all the terrible things that are happening.

Building off of that, Habakkuk is now declaring God isn't just the God of His people's salvation, but God is also the God of his salvation! This is the critical change from his prayer that is also the why behind Habakkuk's joy and ability to continue to worship God.

Habakkuk takes the reality of God working powerfully to save His people and makes it personal. God doesn't just care and intervene to save the nation, but God can and does do the same things in individuals' lives.

Habakkuk knows the power and love God demonstrated previously in awe-inspiring ways is also available to him personally in his present moment. He knows the God who did amazing things for the nation such as splitting the Red Sea and destroying the Egyptian army can use that same power to work in his life and strengthen him personally.

Think about how crazy that is. Think about what a powerful statement Habakkuk is making here. The God who created everything and is powerful enough to, as Habakkuk described in his psalm, crush the heads of His enemies can use the same enormous and unfathomable power to also strengthen and empower him during difficult times. This is why Habakkuk ends his worship proclaiming the reality that God is his strength!

> GOD, the Lord, is my strength; he makes my feet like the deer's; he makes me tread on my high places.
>
> — Habakkuk 3:19

In this verse, Habakkuk describes the reality of God being his strength very poetically. Regardless of the imagery, however, the point is the same. Even though he is struggling and going through a difficult time, Habakkuk knows God is his salvation. He knows God can use the same power and might He showed previously to strengthen and equip him to navigate through everything he is facing.

This is why Habakkuk is able to worship and go as far as to say he will even have joy. This is why Habakkuk isn't interested in ignoring the problems he faced or will face. Again, he sees them as an opportunity for God to show Himself mighty and powerful. It provides him the opportunity to experience personally what God has done throughout history.

What Habakkuk is communicating here is truly incredible. I can't say it enough. For Habakkuk to continue to trust God is noteworthy considering all that has been revealed. But to be able to have joy because you're absolutely convinced that even the terrible things in your life are just another opportunity for

God to show Himself great and worthy of all worship shows the kind of faith Habakkuk had. It is a testament to this prophet's faith and his commitment to go forward living his life consistent with that faith.

More Than Happily Ever After

This is how the book fittingly ends. But as you read the last words, this ending probably won't be described by many as a neat and tidy "happily ever after." If you know your history, you know the Babylonians do eventually invade just as God said they would. This means what Habakkuk feared and prayed against does happen. So while the book may not end like many of our favorite fairy tales, I would argue its ending is much more compelling and meaningful. Instead of Habakkuk getting what he prayed for, the book ends with what was a dejected and vexed prophet worshipping God because of His sufficiency.

Now, I realize there may be some who think it is strange to celebrate the current ending over and against Habakkuk's prayers being answered. If we were in Habakkuk's position, I am sure all of us would rather receive what we were praying for. That's obviously understandable, but what Habakkuk demonstrates instead is something worth our attention—we must be people who worship regardless of the circumstances.

Here is something we all absolutely need to remember—worship is the antidote to so much of what ails us both spiritually and temporally. In my life, there were countless times when I was feeling down or feeling as if there wasn't much in the way of hope until I started to worship God. And guess what happened as I worshipped? Things changed.

Now, my circumstances or what was bothering me hadn't

changed. But I did. My attitude and outlook became completely different. I was no longer down and even, at times, had a good attitude compared to how I was before. That is the power of worship, and Habakkuk demonstrates it in a magnificent way. He went from questioning and complaining to worshipping God and having joy—truly a remarkable change. Again, this is the power that results from worship.

It could and maybe should be asked, however, how can something as simple as worship have such a powerful effect? How can it turn moments of sadness and pain like those the prophet felt completely around?

It goes all the way back to how we were created. As I talked about in the pride chapter, we as humans were made to respond in reverence and adoration when we experience God and the attributes of who He is, such as His power, magnificence, revelation, and the awe-inspiring nature of how He created everything. This is worship, and this is our rightful response to God.

When discussing this topic, though, it is important to realize what flows naturally from our worship—a focus on God and His glory. It is impossible for us to worship God without having our focus move to Him, what He has done, and what He can do. When we worship God as He created us to do, it means we are responding to Him and who He is, so there is no way to worship God that does not exalt Him and His attributes. We cannot rightfully worship God if He isn't being lifted up and magnified.

All of this is important to recognize because of how it affects us. It does not matter whether we start by thinking of God and His greatness (and that leads us to worship Him) or we start worshipping God only to be led back to how great and glorious He is; the result is the same because it's what always happens when we worship—our focus moves off ourselves and our circumstances and onto God instead.

Are you getting how important and powerful that is? To

demonstrate, look again at Habakkuk. What does he say causes him to rejoice and have joy? It is the God of his salvation and strength. It is God who demonstrated His love and power previously and now offers that same love and power to him personally. This is Habakkuk's focus now. It's what allows him to have joy and is the foundation of his worship.

With that statement, Habakkuk makes it clear his focus has moved off the Babylonians and onto how great and powerful God is instead. Now, this isn't to say he is ignoring the impending disaster. As we saw, that isn't the case at all. He is well aware of what's coming, but his prayer and worship have refocused him. Throughout the entire book, Habakkuk had been focused on things other than God. At first, it was the wickedness and injustice all around him. Later in the book, it was the Babylonians and the coming invasion. Now, however, Habakkuk's gaze is firmly fixed on God.

His shift in perspective highlights this important fact—the horrible things that will happen do not compare to the God he serves. This is why Habakkuk can say he will rejoice and have joy. This is why he can confidently declare God will be his strength despite the wickedness all around him and the impending disaster.

Habakkuk's final lesson to us shows how we can join him by having joy even in the middle of the worst moments and most difficult times of our lives. How? By worshipping God. Even when you don't feel like it or can't begin to imagine doing something like worshipping in your current circumstances, worship anyway.

To be clear, I am not saying it will make everything better. Like Habakkuk, you will often find your situation hasn't changed at all. But that isn't the point, is it? God never promised us everything we face will always turn out how we want. He hasn't even promised us we will always be blessed (despite what so many preachers today say). The reason for this is that God isn't interested in simply having everything go our way.

Instead, God is interested in who we are becoming as we walk through those difficult times and tough seasons. God has His own plan for all of history and our lives, and it will certainly clash with what we want at times. That is why God isn't worried about whether we would sign off on the outcome or not.

What God is truly interested in is transforming us and transforming us specifically into His image (2 Cor. 3:18). This means God knows what is important isn't for us to get all the answers or outcomes we desire. What *is* important is experiencing more of Him because that is the thing that will ultimately transform us.

As we experience more of God and, as a result, come to know Him to a greater degree, it keeps us from being people who are thrown to and fro (Eph. 4:14) by anything and everything that comes our way. Rather, we can be people who stand firm in faith and trust in God. We can be people who have joy regardless of what we face.

And it all comes back to worship. Sure, there are other ways all of this can happen, but I believe worship is one of the greatest ways for us to experience more of God regardless of who we are and what we are facing. I also believe it is one of the most effective ways to have joy even in the middle of our worst circumstances and darkest valley.

As we discussed, when we worship God, we cannot help but have our focus become fixed on who He is, His power, and what He has done. This results in the same realization that Habakkuk had so many years ago—God is greater than any of our circumstances and anything we could ever face.

This is the ending we are left with. We aren't left with answered prayers. No, what we are left with is a distraught prophet worshipping God. And what a beautiful ending it is. I love that this is the last image we get. In a book about questioning God and even struggling with His will at times, it is fitting the final word is one of worship. It is fitting we leave not with "happily ever after," but we leave with a knowledge of how God is greater.

Your Final Word

As this book draws to a close, I'd encourage you to let worship be the final word in your story or circumstances. Now, I'm not going to pretend this recommendation will be easy for so many. I know it won't. There are undoubtedly some who are reading this and can hardly wrap their heads around worshipping in the middle of what they're going through.

Isn't that the beautiful thing about how Habakkuk's story ends, though? Nothing has changed for Habakkuk except himself. I'll repeat that. Nothing has changed for Habakkuk except himself.

He changed, not his circumstances. His ending is one of joy instead of fear and disillusionment, and it had nothing to do with his situation changing. He is now able to rejoice instead of being haunted by questions regarding what God is doing and His plan.

I think we should all follow Habakkuk's example and choose to worship in the midst of our difficulties. Again, your situation might not change. As a matter of fact, for many, it may be impossible for things to change. Whatever it is you are facing, I can guarantee one thing, though—if you worship, even for a few short moments, you will change. Your focus will move off of your circumstances and onto the God who is greater than them. Your focus can move off of what is impossible and onto the one who is the God of the impossible. You might even be able to join Habakkuk by feeling joy in the midst of your circumstances.

If you don't even know where to begin worshipping with what you're facing, like Habakkuk, start with recognizing what God has done throughout history. Open your Bible and find stories of His greatness. Have your heart lifted by how He has been able to work miracles and good outcomes out of even the most dire and impossible of situations.

Then take all of that and again follow Habakkuk's lead by making it personal. Join him in realizing that God isn't just the God of the past, but He can and does work powerfully to deliver His followers even today. God has never been confined to stories that took place thousands of years ago. He is the same God He has always been, and that means He is working today just as He was when we read about Him saving, healing, and intervening in miraculous ways in the lives of His people.

Be convinced the same power God demonstrated over and over again can strengthen and equip you to navigate through your dark valley. Join Habakkuk in seeing your struggles as an opportunity for God to show Himself mighty once again. Let worship help you view your troubles as an opportunity to experience personally what God has done powerfully and miraculously throughout history.

Let your mind and heart be taken to all God has done for you. Even if you feel like that list isn't very long, maybe look at one last instance where God was questioned, and it is the most poignant question ever asked of God: "My God, my God, why have you forsaken me?"

If you aren't familiar with this question, it was the question Jesus cried out to the Father on the cross before He died (Matt. 27:46, Mk. 15:34). And it is both a powerful and significant question.

Through the brutality of what Jesus encountered, He cries

out to the Father as He experiences something genuinely incomprehensible and even more brutal than His torture—separation in His relationship from the rest of the Trinity with whom He has been in perfect relationship for all of eternity. But why? Why did Jesus experience this?

He was experiencing all of this for us. You see, Jesus stepped down from the glories of heaven and became a man—the perfect man. He lived His life without sin and in complete obedience and submission to God. His life was everything ours should be but never could be because of sin. So, Jesus lived a righteous life while we do not. He deserved God's blessing and reward for the life He lived while we deserve punishment and eternal separation from God for our prideful rebellion against Him.

But what happened instead? On the cross, Jesus took the punishment we deserved in order for us to receive the reward that He earned. He died in our place so that we could have eternal life and be made righteous. And a paramount moment as Jesus took our punishment on the cross was being separated from the Father.

There is plenty of debate surrounding the nature of how Jesus was separated from the rest of the Trinity and for how long if He was. But whatever was happening at that moment was enough to cause Jesus to echo the infamous words of Psalm 22 that take the form of questioning God. With all of the horrible things He went through physically, what He was experiencing at that moment caused Jesus such tremendous anguish.

It is a powerful scene, and it demonstrates magnificently to all of us how much God loves us. That He loved us enough to give up His only son to experience something so unimaginable as He died for our sins is truly hard to grasp. The beautiful thing about all of this is that, as a result of Jesus' perfect sacrifice and His resurrection, everyone who is in Christ never has to worry about being separated from God again. For all of eternity, we will be with God and in His presence. Jesus on the cross experienced being forsaken so that we as Christians never have to worry about being forsaken by God.

You see, looking at this moment should be simultaneously heartbreaking and mind-blowing to all of us. We should all feel crushed that our sin resulted in what Jesus had to bear on the cross while also being blown away that He loved us enough to willingly do it.

We should also be encouraged by this particular scene within the crucifixion narrative. If you are in a place where you are questioning God, it is hard to think of anything that can lead to more hope and encouragement than looking at Jesus crying out on the cross. When we are in those dark times where we're questioning God, we can always know Jesus sympathizes with us and our weakness (Heb. 4:15).

So if you have nothing else, you have that. If you can't think of a single reason to worship God, think of that moment—think of how infinitely valuable you are to Him that He would do something so extraordinary for you so that He could spend eternity with you.

Once your focus has moved to God and what He has done, respond to it however you can. This is the heart of worship, and it is what we all need when we are in the middle of situations and circumstances where we find ourselves questioning God.

The amazing thing about how this biblical book ends is that it offers us to have our story end the same way. We can always choose to continue to question God and rail against Him and what He is doing around us and in our lives. Or like Habakkuk, we can choose to live by faith. We can choose to trust God and His promise that He is doing something in our day (and our lives) we wouldn't believe even if we were told.

And we can have the many stories of our lives end with

worship. Even as we walk through the worst life can throw at us, we can join this little-known prophet by having joy because we know our God is greater and more powerful than anything we could ever face. We can have the last word for our circumstances be that of worship instead of questions like, "What are you doing, God?"

DISCUSSION QUESTIONS

Chapter 1

-Have you ever questioned the circumstances or situations that were happening in your life?

-If you are a Christian, have you ever found yourself in a place that, like Job, you were questioning God?

-Did you know what a lament was before reading this chapter? Do you think laments are important?

-Do you agree with Bo that unanswered prayer and a lack of intervention by God are two of the most common reasons we question God? What are some other reasons that cause us to question God?

-Like Habakkuk, have either of those things (unanswered prayer and lack of intervention by God) ever frustrated you as you followed God?

Chapter 2

-Have you ever learned something important after talking to someone else by looking deeper into what he or she said?

-Do you try to find deeper meaning or lessons in other parts of life?

-Have you ever been in a situation where your focus began to get limited to what you were experiencing or going through? Did you lose touch with other parts of life? Looking back, was that a positive or negative thing?

-Do you think there are times when a change of perspective is necessary to help us move beyond ourselves and see the greater picture? Have you ever had one of those times?

-Do you feel God has ever challenged you to expand your focus and change your perspective as He did with Habakkuk?

-Do you believe God is at work all around you even if you don't see or understand it? How can that affect your focus or perspective?

-What are some ways that help you readjust your focus and perspective?

Chapter 3

-What are some of your favorite promises in the Bible? Did you know about God's promise to Habakkuk?

-What do you think about the statements, "We can't hope to genuinely grasp all [God] is doing in our situations. [...] it is foolish to assume we can even begin to fathom all God is doing in the world."? Do you agree or disagree?

-What are your thoughts on this statement, "Not only is God always working in our lives and everything we are seeing and experiencing, but ... whatever God is up to would be mind-blowing if we found out."? Do you find that encouraging?

-How do you think accepting your limitations will help you as you walk through this life? Do you think it can help us not be riddled with fear, worry, and uncertainty when we don't have to be? Have there ever been times when you think this lesson would have helped you as you faced difficulties?

-Do you think the promise given to Habakkuk can be a place where you can draw strength during hard times?

Chapter 4

- Are you someone who likes to be in control? Are you someone who likes to have their life planned out? What was your reaction when things felt out of your control or weren't going how you planned?

- Was there ever a time in your life where you had this thought or something similar, "If I only knew what God was doing..."? Why do you think knowing what God is up to in our situations would help if it would at all?

-What do you think of Habakkuk's reaction to God's plan? How do you think you would have reacted if you were in his place?

- Has there ever been a time in your life where you struggled to accept what God was doing? Why?

- Has there ever been a time in your life when you looked back and agreed with Joseph that what was meant for evil God meant for good? Has that changed how you view the different circumstances and situations you face?

- How do you think you can take the lesson of trusting God's plan and apply it to your life?

Chapter 5

- Would you describe yourself as being patient? What are some things that make you impatient?

- Have there been times when you have been impatient and there was no need to be?

- Be honest, have you ever been impatient with God? Has there ever been a time when His timing was different than yours?

- Has something ever happened to you later that you did not expect would happen? Did you give up on it or just assume it wouldn't happen?

- How do you think you can be more patient in your life and walk with God?

Chapter 6

- What are some things you have chased after in your life thinking it would provide fulfillment or satisfaction? Did it? Are you completely satisfied in your life as a result?

- What is pride? Do you understand how it is connected to our worship?

- Did you know that pride was part of the first temptation?

- Have you noticed pride in your life? If so, how?

- Have there been times when you have elevated what you wanted or thought above God's will and way? If so, what was the result?

- Is there something you learned in this chapter that you did not know before?

Chapter 7

- Do you understand why God put righteousness and faith together?

- Do you see the difference between a person living by faith and one living in pride? What are some of those differences?

- Is there an example of faith in the Bible that is your favorite? If so, why?

- We know that we have the same choice Habakkuk had, so

has there ever been a time when you took the path of the proud person instead of the righteous person?

- What are some things you can do to live more by faith?

Chapter 8

- Have you ever had to make a decision(s) in your life that had a tremendous effect on it? When you look back, would you make a different decision?

- What are your thoughts on prayer? When you think about praying to God, what comes to mind?

- Has God ever answered any of your prayers?

- Have you ever prayed selfishly? Have you ever prayed for something and looked back later only to realize that you were trying to get God to give you your will instead of His?

- Do you think you could pray a prayer of submission like Habakkuk prayed? Why or why not?

- What are some ways we can work on submitting to God?

Chapter 9

- Is there something that came to mind when Bo discussed disappointing endings? If so, how did the ending affect everything else in your mind?

- What do you think when you think of worship? If you worship, what does your worship usually look like?

- Do you agree that even your difficulties and tough circumstances can be an opportunity to experience personally what God has done powerfully throughout history?

- When you worship God, do you find your focus is drawn to Him over other things? If so, do you think this could be valuable when you are facing difficulties?

- Would you like your story and the story of each and every

circumstance you face to end like Habakkuk's story? Do you think you could ever find joy even in the middle of your difficulties? How do you think both of these things can happen?

www.ingramcontent.com/pod-product-compliance
Lightning Source LLC
Chambersburg PA
CBHW071500070426
42452CB00041B/1943